Embracing Support

7 Strategies to a Happy Empowered Amazing Life

By Claudia R. Seiler-Mutton
RN, BScN, MEd

Embracing Support Copyright © 2020 Claudia R. Seiler-Mutton

All rights reserved. No part of this book may be reproduced by any mechanical, photographic, or electronic process, or in the form of phonographic recording; nor may it be stored in a retrieval system, transmitted, or otherwise copied for public or private use without the prior written permission of the publisher.

The author of this book does not dispense medical advice or prescribe the use of any technique as a form of treatment for physical, emotional, or medical problems without the advice of a physician or other trained health care professional, either directly or indirectly. The intent of the author is only to offer information of a general nature to help the reader in their quest for emotional and spiritual well-being. In the event that the reader uses any of the information in this book, as is their constitutional right, the author and publisher assume no responsibility for the reader's actions.

DreamScapes
Edmonton, AB, Canada
info@HealWithSupport.com

Cover art: Heather Morin
Seven Domains of Internal Support Diagram design: Sonja Mutton

ISBN 978-1-9992703-1-5   eBook
ISBN 978-1-9992703-0-8   Paperback

First Edition

This is a work of nonfiction. Some names and identifying details have been changed.

A percentage of proceeds from this book go to support the Edmonton WIN House (previously known as the Edmonton Women's Shelter) and the Edmonton Kids Kottage. For information about or to donate to these organizations, visit https://winhouse.org/ and https://www.kidskottage.org/.

To my loving husband, Harold: You are my rock and my safe place to land. Thank you for letting me dream and fly.

To Sonja and Alexandria: You are my angels. Thank you for showing me how simple it is to unconditionally love and be loved.

To the rest of my wonderful family: You are my support system. Thank you for your unconditional support and faith in me. You believed in me even when I didn't, and beyond anything else, that kept me going and taught me to ask for and accept support.

Above all, to my mom: You are my teacher. Thank you for your guidance. Although we sometimes disagreed on the right path, I wouldn't be where I am today if you hadn't pointed me in this direction. I know you did the best you could with what you had. Always.

"The secret of change is to focus all of your energy, not on fighting the old, but on building the new."

∞ ***Socrates*** ∞
The Peaceful Warrior (Film)

Acknowledgments

A project of this magnitude can only come together with the support of countless amazing people whose invaluable support, love, and guidance brought this dream to fruition. I often get so overwhelmed at the thought of how far this book project has come that the right words to express how immensely grateful I am don't come to me. I hope the following will suffice.

I would like to thank:

- ∞ Jordan, Jared, Jannette, Suze, and Ali for your love, encouragement, and insight into my limiting beliefs and your guidance to help me work through and replace those beliefs with more supportive ones.
- ∞ Jay Fiset and Rae-ann Wood-Schatz for "poking" at my Belief System (BS) and giving me an opportunity to see infinite possibilities and dream bigger, without ever questioning my ability to achieve those dreams.
- ∞ My co-workers who have supported and believed in me. Your belief in my ability to write and create a book like this has been unbelievably motivating.
- ∞ My support team and editors: The team at Big Sky Author Services (Zoey, Sarah, Jim, and Heather) led by Tammy Plunkett; Theresa Agnew Professional Writing Services; and Karen Rowe at Front Rowe Seat. Your insights, suggestions, corrections, and patience have allowed this project to evolve to completion, and have let me get my message across clearly and concisely. Words fail me to express my magnitude of thanks.

- The Grant MacEwan University Centre for the Advancement of Faculty Excellence, under the direction of the Faculty Development Committee, for its financial support from the Divisional Faculty Development funds, which were applied towards the editorial costs.
- Tammy Johnston at the Financial Guides for her eternal love, drive, support, and all the connections a person would ever need. Thanks, too, for calling me on my BS.
- The boys of Nickelback. Your music and drive inspired and motivated me to keep writing when I thought about giving up, and saved my sanity more times than I can count. Keep doing what you do best.
- To the many personal growth and development authors who continue to share their thoughts and ideas with the world for your guidance and belief in an enlightened and empowered humanity.
- Above all else, my family and friends for putting up with my moods, my quirks, my busy-ness, and my craziness as I was working on my dreams. Thank you for teaching me what unconditional love and support truly are.

Contents

Introduction 1
   Why is Support so Important? 5
Strategy 1: Get Clear on What You Have (Defining Support) 11
   What Does Support Mean to Me? 11
      Why Don't We Ask for Support? 18
      Additional Reasons for Not Asking for or Accepting Support 21
   Beware of Knights in Shining Armor 26
   Good Fences Make Good Neighbors 28
   How Does Support Translate into Everyday Life? 35
      Role Models 36
   Getting the Right Kind of Support 38
      Activity: A Personal View of Support 41
      Dream Big 44
   A Few Last Points about Being Clear 45
      Activity: My Contrast List 49
Strategy 2: Get Clear on What You Want (Accepting Support) 52
   Why Don't I Have What I Want? 52
   Reclaim Your Power 53
   Ask the Right Person (The Right Way and at the Right Time) 57

The Right Person 58
    Activity: Getting Clear About Support 59
    Right Person, Wrong Support 63
The Right Way 67
The Right Time 69
    Take a Break 70
    When to Ask for Support 73
    Activity: Stress Reduction 75
Control 77
    Finding Support 79
    Activity: Getting Support Plan 80

Strategy 3: Get Focused on What's Stopping You (Understanding Beliefs and Accountability) 84
    What are Beliefs? 84
    Our Beliefs Act like Jars 86
    The Birth of Beliefs 87
    "Those Who Love Me, Leave Me" 89
    "I Don't Deserve to be Loved" 91
    The Wake-Up Call 93
    Foundational Beliefs: A Snapshot 96
    Changing Our Ways 98
    Activity: Discovering Foundational Beliefs . 100
    Moving Forward with Change 104

Seven Steps to Accountability 105

Activity: Seven Steps to Accountability 109

Pulling it all Together 114

Accountability 114

Strategy 4: Become Empowered (Understanding How Beliefs Affect Support) 119

Fear and Support 119

"I'm Not Good Enough" 121

Moving Forward with Support 123

Trust and Support 124

A Matter of Choice 128

How Beliefs Affect Support 129

"I Have Nothing of Value to Contribute" 129

"I'm Not Wanted" 132

The Upside 134

Activity: Beliefs and Support 136

A Different Perspective: Asking for Support 140

Activity: Time to Reflect 142

How Can I Change my Beliefs to Create More Support? 152

Activity: Visualization 153

Strategy 5: Change Old Behavior Patterns (Creating New Habits with Support) 157

Activity: Identifying Behavior Patterns........159

Is It Working?...161

  Breaking Down the Patterns.........................162

What Would You Like to Change?...................165

  Activity: Achieving Your Ideal....................165

Ask Anyway..169

Firing Your Support...171

  The Unsolicited Supporter............................176

  Activity: Evaluating Support........................177

A Few Thoughts on Stress Behavior Patterns..181

  A Reflection: How We Experience Time.....182

  Stress Management Basics...........................183

  Activity: Seven Steps to Stress
  Management..190

  Act As If..200

Strategy 6: Take Charge and Put your Plan into Action (A Step-by-Step Plan for Creating More Support)...204

  What's Stopping You from Having Support?..206

  Activity: Another Kick at the Beliefs Can....206

  More on Challenging Your Beliefs...............208

  Your Amazing Strategies in Action................210

  Getting the Support You Want......................225

Strategy 7: Take Care of Yourself (The Most Vital Support) 227

    Beliefs and Internal Support 231

    The Next Generation 232

    Learning to Support Myself 233

    Setting Priorities 234

    A Reflection about Scarcity and Abundance 237

    Calling all Caregivers 238

    "Sharpening the Saw" 239

    Mix It Up! 241

    A Reflection about Procrastination 242

  The Seven Domains of Internal Support 243

    The Physical Domain of Internal Support 243

  The Seven Domains of Internal Support Diagram 247

    The Intellectual/Mental Domain of Internal Support 248

    The Emotional Domain of Internal Support . 251

    The Spiritual Domain of Internal Support 254

    The Financial/Occupational Domain of Internal Support 257

    The Environmental Domain of Internal Support 261

    The Social Domain of Internal Support 265

Activity: Pulling it all Together....................268
Celebrate Success...273
Every End Is a New Beginning 276
In Honor of My Mom 280
References and Resources 287
About the Author 289

Introduction

"To get something you've never had, you have to do something you've never done before."
∞ *Unknown* ∞

Once upon a time, in the Kingdom of I Can Do It All By Myself, there lived a beautiful, sophisticated, intelligent, and independent princess. She was amazing. She was a wife and mother, a full-time nursing instructor, and a casual-shift nurse at the local hospital. She volunteered at her children's school and supported many local charities. She ran the kingdom with a firm hand, making sure her family was well cared for and well-fed, with enough groceries, fresh laundry, and a clean castle. She also made sure her students had all they needed to be successful in their studies. All were well-coddled and lived a life of luxury under her rule.

There was a problem, however, with the "happily-ever-after." Over time, the Princess ended up doing more and more for her family, students, and patients. She worked hard day and night, with no one to help her. Because she had been doing these things for so long, no one questioned whether she might need some help. They just accepted these things would be done for them. In fact, they started taking it all for granted. But there was simply too much for the Princess to do all by herself. Laundry started piling up, dirty dishes were left in the sink, and term papers didn't get marked. Her two little princesses went without baths and turned into trolls who played under the drawbridge. The fences at the kingdom's borders were neglected and became overrun by the neighbors' sheep and the Princess' own pesky relatives. The kingdom was in dire straits.

Now, the Princess was not the type of person to give up easily. She kept trying and trying, and managed (somewhat successfully) to run the kingdom. But at what cost? You see, by keeping such tight control over her kingdom, the Princess effectively cut off anyone who could help her along the way. After all, she thought, no one could run the kingdom as well as she could. But her unwavering commitment to doing it all by herself did not serve anyone.

Her husband, the Prince, was frustrated because the Princess wouldn't let him help look after the trolls or the castle. Her mother, the Queen, felt alienated. Her students were annoyed because their papers weren't getting marked and they had no feedback on how to improve their nursing practice. However, the Princess may have had it the worst of all—she felt the Queen was judging her, she felt discouraged because she had no time for herself, and she felt her students thought she wasn't a good enough instructor. She was utterly exhausted and getting depressed because of her perceived lack of motivation. She knew she had alienated her family because she forgot how to just love the trolls and the Prince, and she was so overwhelmed and alone that she

Embracing Support

felt like she just couldn't go on anymore.

In short, the Princess was miserable. Often, she wished for a knight in shining armor to come and rescue her. Worst of all, she felt unsupported, abandoned, and taken for granted. Even though many people in her kingdom could have, and even wanted, to help her, she didn't know how to ask for and accept their support. The Princess thought it would be a sign of weakness to ask, or that she would be rejected if she did ask. She felt her subjects would think her an incapable ruler, so she continued to struggle on her own. She even began to think about giving up her crown and running away from her family and her kingdom. Eventually, she felt so low and so weak that she didn't even know what she wanted anymore. It was all too overwhelming.

Then one day her Personal Development Fairy Godfather came to visit. He gave the Princess a good poke in her belief system. "Is it really true that you have to do everything on your own?" he asked. His question upset the Princess beyond reason, because it was so very obvious and she didn't like hearing the truth about what she thought she was going through. She ranted and raved and screamed and cried.

Finally, she calmed down enough to start thinking logically. "Why do I feel like I have to do this all on my own? Why don't I ask for—or accept—the support that is so abundantly available to me? Why don't I even see the support when it's offered?" After all, all she wanted was a happy, empowered, and amazing life. Wouldn't asking for support only help her along the way?

Then and there she made a decision. The Princess knew the road would be rocky at first, but she also knew that learning to accept the support others offered provided the key she needed to open the door to her happiness. Only if she learned to ask for and accept the support around her would she be able to create the life for herself she'd been dreaming about. Because with support, she would finally have the power to heal.

The End . . . ?

Not by a long shot. It only gets better from here.

If you asked the Princess today what she sees as the most wonderful thing about her new life, she'd tell you she now has peace and love in her kingdom and that it almost runs itself. In fact, her loyal subjects decided to rename the Kingdom of I Can Do It All By Myself. It is now known as the Kingdom of We Create Amazing Things Together. Today, she has the time to take her dreams off the shelf—the ones she'd put on hold during the busy times—and start turning them into reality. She's even started dreaming new dreams—ones she was too afraid to consider before she had support. All because she learned about asking for, accepting, and allowing support into her life. And the best part was, asking got easier, every time she tried.

Can you relate to the poor, tired, overwhelmed Princess from the Kingdom of I Can Do It All By Myself? Perhaps you rule your kingdom in a similar fashion? Have you ever felt so completely overwhelmed or alone that you just wanted to run away and start a new life? Maybe you've felt frustrated and let down, or like no one heard you when you asked for help. Or maybe you felt taken for granted. You give and you give, but when you need someone, no one's around to help? Think of a time where you may have wanted a knight in shining armor (or perhaps a fairy godfather) to rescue you from your troubles or worries. You may have given the world to hear them say, "Let me take this burden off your shoulders."

If you're reading this book, I suspect you can relate to the Princess' story on some level, and you've had times in your life when you've been just as unhappy as she was. What did you do at those times? Did you reach out for support and ask for what you needed? Did you ask, but not get what you wanted? Did you avoid the situation altogether and do something else instead? Are you still struggling with trying to do everything on your own?

This particular princess figured out the key to creating a happy, empowered, and amazing life, and all it took was for her to learn how to ask for—and accept—support. "Easier said than done," you say? Not really. It's actually quite simple. And the most amazing thing is, support is abundantly available to you: the more you learn to ask for support, the more you'll find around you.

Why is Support so Important?

What is support—and why would I decide to write an entire book about it?

As you have probably guessed, I am that princess in the story, and asking for and accepting support was something I struggled with for many years. I know I'm not the only one with these experiences. I've worked as a nurse for more than two decades, and I see my colleagues, my patients and clients, their family members, my nursing students, and other members of the health care team become overwhelmed, yet neither ask for nor accept support. And this isn't the case just in the helping professions. I see it everywhere, all the time. As a parent and teacher, I know there are different perspectives on what it means to be supported or not supported, but the bottom line is we all need support.

In conversations with friends and acquaintances, I have heard many different definitions of support and many different views on whether people need it or not. Some comments have included:

"Why would people want or need support? I manage very well on my own."

"Asking for support means I'm weak, while doing everything for myself independently means I'm strong and powerful."

"I'm smart enough to figure things out on my own."

"I have all the support I could ever want or need."

In listening to these conversations, I realized having support is much more than simply asking for what I think I want or need and accepting help from others. I have learned support is also about relationships and interactions with ourselves and others, and I often feel much more supported after I've had a chance to just sit and visit and laugh with friends or family. I also learned I need to be clear about the type of support I ask for or accept. But most importantly, I've learned how to change my own thoughts and circumstances to create more support for myself.

Once I realized support would be an immensely positive addition to my life, the next step was to follow through and ask the right person, at the right time. I have learned that just wishing for a happier, more empowered life doesn't cut it. It takes some work, and it's much easier to get there with support. In fact, in order to live a truly happy and empowered life, support and connection to self and others is critical.

When I started paying attention to my own life, I learned that in order to feel truly supported and passionate about life, I needed to make sure I looked after and supported myself first. **If I neglected myself, the support I received from others wouldn't change my circumstances.** Instead, I'd keep re-creating the same conditions for myself, living through the same frustrating situations, over and over and over again.

If I truly wanted to live the easier, more passionate life I deserved, I also needed to look after myself, and I needed to connect with others to support me along the way. We all do. It's part of being human. And let's just be clear that supporting ourselves does not mean we have to neglect others. It's not a "them or me" kind of game. It can, in fact, be completely win-win. It may take a little while to get there, so give yourself a chance to learn. Without support, I would have a tough time managing my two girls and contributing to a stable family income. I would be challenged to maintain my home, and I would never have been able to write this book. Without support, my life would be back to the frustrating struggle it once was. Please trust me when I say I much prefer the new happier, more empowered life I've created for myself. The life with support.

Support is something each and every one of us could use more of in our lives, no doubt about it. Many of us struggle on a daily basis with all we feel we have to do in a day. In Western culture it often feels like very few supports are in place to help make life easier, or to help us cope with our day-to-day lives. By being so focused on *doing*, we forget how to *be* and to enjoy living.

Now, I'm not saying it isn't possible to get by without support. I know it's possible, and many of us do it every day. I've been there myself, and managed quite nicely . . . for a time. I'm just saying that once I learned how to ask for and accept support, the struggle ended. I was able to start enjoying the important things in life: my family, my home, my creativity—because I started to work as part of a team. This meant I had time to take breaks along the way and to start doing some of the beautiful, creative things that rejuvenate my soul.

When I was at the height of ruling the Kingdom of I Can Do It All By Myself, a happy, empowered, amazing life felt entirely out of reach. I was definitely not happy and often felt anxious and overwhelmed. I felt that I had little choice or control over my own life, because I was constantly doing something rather than actually living in the moment. I thought I had to do it all on my own. The truth is, though, we don't have to do it alone. In these pages, you'll find you have an amazing support system at your disposal and you'll

Embracing Support

learn to effectively use all the tools you need to HEAL. Through self-awareness, you'll see that you have a choice, and in consciously choosing who you want to be and what you want your life to look like, you'll learn that you have the power to choose the life you've dreamed about.

I will share some very basic concepts in seven main Strategies that will help you understand what support is all about and how the beliefs you have about yourself and your world affect how much support you have in your life. We'll define support and I'll invite you to think about your personal views on the subject. Then we'll walk through a step-by-step process for creating the support you want and need. Throughout, I'll ask questions, and if you answer them honestly and do the work, you'll come away with a much greater awareness of why you live your life the way you do and how it could potentially be better. In other words, this book supports you in HEALing your life.

One note for consideration before we begin. Change can be scary and create anxiety for some individuals. Because we're talking about beliefs and how they affect our lives, you may find yourself struggling with or even resisting some of concepts I'm describing. This is a perfectly normal response to learning something new and potentially uncomfortable. As you'll learn, our beliefs are created to protect us and don't particularly like to be challenged. I encourage you to be gentle with yourself, and to give yourself the opportunity to broaden your thoughts and beliefs about your world and your place in it. Be honest with yourself, and use this feeling of discomfort or resistance as an indicator that you may have just triggered a belief which may be keeping you stuck in your current situation. It's safe to examine this belief or these thoughts, and then you get to decide whether you want to hold on to the belief or if it may be time for some new beliefs that may lead to different results in your life. When you realize a belief has been poked or triggered, it will be a perfect opportunity to practice asking for support. There are several examples coming up, including my own challenges in changing some of my beliefs. I survived, and have grown as a person because of it, and so can you, if you're willing to challenge yourself a little bit.

Are you ready to start on your journey to living a Happy, Empowered, Amazing Life?

"If I have the belief that I can do it, I shall surely acquire the capacity to do it even if I may not have it at the beginning."
∞ **Mahatma Gandhi** ∞

Strategy 1: Get Clear on What You Have (Defining Support)

"Abundance is not something we acquire. It is something we tune into."
∞ *Dr. Wayne Dyer* ∞

A quick look in the dictionary gives several definitions for "support," but none of them fully encompass this essential piece of a happy and empowered life. One definition refers to the physical act of propping up, carrying, and sustaining something. Most of the time, allowing support into our lives doesn't mean we need someone to piggyback us to safety, and only seeing support in this way can make a person feel like asking for support is only for emergencies. That's not quite what we're looking for with support. Another definition gets a little closer to my idea about support. It identifies support as encouragement, helping, defending, cheering, and assistance. However, **support is about more than just helping each other.**

What Does Support Mean to Me?

Let's define "support" as **a way to empower individuals to use the strength and love from others to create something miraculous for themselves.** Support is knowing that someone is in your corner; someone you can rely or lean on and share your burden with. Support means that you don't have to go through a struggle alone. Sometimes, yes, I may need the strength of others to hold me up, but for the most part, support is a way to feel strong and find a way together. A technical definition of having support is **a means whereby an individual experiences an empowered physical, emotional, and psychological state that lets them experience love and living their life's purpose**. When we are supported, we feel encouraged, hopeful, and lighter, and we are surrounded by others who care. It means that we no longer feel like we have to carry the weight of the world on our own. We are not so overwhelmed by all we feel we have to do. In other words, having support allows you to work toward accomplishing anything you set your mind and heart to, and when you are supported, you have the assistance you need to deal with a situation without having someone come in and rescue you from the mess you may have created.

If you've ever struggled in your life or felt overwhelmed by a situation, you know what it's like to not have enough support. If you've lived without adequate support for a long time, you may even think this is a normal way of life. And if this is the case, now may be the time to ask yourself: "Am I happy with my life as it is? Do I wish that parts of any given day could be simpler or less difficult?" Or maybe you say to yourself, "There has got to be an easier way!"

I used to do that all the time. Things changed significantly, though, after I started asking for and accepting support. Before we get there though, let me tell you a story that will help you start to think about your own definition of support.

Several years ago, I took a personal development

Embracing Support

course on entrepreneurship in Calgary, Alberta, facilitated by Jay Fiset of the Creators Code. I had known Jay for about 10 years from various other courses I had taken, and I always ended up leaving the seminars with amazing insights and a new perspective on life. Thus, when I wanted to expand my coaching business, it seemed only natural for me to take the entrepreneur boot camp weekend Jay was offering.

That weekend, there were 30 or 40 of us in our rows of chairs in the small hotel conference room, all eagerly watching Jay at the front of the room as his charismatic storytelling drew us in and brought old dreams and new possibilities to the forefront. He imparted new information and then had us work through some related exercises. As is normal human behavior, I heard loudest what was most important to me at the time. When he discussed what it takes to become a successful entrepreneur, Jay inadvertently "poked at," or triggered, some of my subconscious beliefs about entrepreneurship. My immediate reaction to his very straightforward information about marketing using social media was: "I can't do that! I don't have enough time. I don't know how to use any of those sites. I can't . . . I don't know enough. I'm not good enough. I'll never succeed. May as well not even try." Although the information was very basic, it impacted me immensely, as so many of my limiting beliefs about what I was capable of in business were triggered, and my frustration mounted with each subconscious thought. All I saw was reason after reason why I would not be successful in business, because of what I didn't know. And not once did I even consider what role asking for and accepting other people's assistance, intelligence, or advice played in being successful in business, as well as my life in general.

After the learning activity, the group broke for lunch. The emotional impact of the belief poke was so strong that I didn't want to go back and finish the course. While others were getting to know each other and networking, I spent my lunch hour isolated from the group and angry. Then and there I realized I would never be able to establish a successful business on my own. Unconsciously, I equated that thought with failure and asked myself again, "Why even try?" The importance of support in creating a successful business was so foreign to me that I gave up on my dream before it had a chance to blossom. I felt hurt, lonely, and abandoned as I realized how often I needed support and just didn't ask for it—or didn't accept it, even if it was offered. How often did I struggle at work to solve a problem, because I should know how to do that on my own? How often was my family not able to help with laundry clean up, because it had to be done my way? How often did I get frustrated with not having enough time to exercise or clean up the clutter, because I didn't have boundaries on my time or a system in place so others could help? How often did I feel completely overwhelmed by my never ending to-do list?

Not being one to give up on something I've put effort into, I faced my emotions. I did go back after lunch, but didn't get much out of the rest of the day because I was so focused on my own thoughts and issues. I asked myself, "Why do I try to do everything on my own instead of asking for help?" I knew very well that I had many people in my life who were willing to support me and make life a little easier. I realized I often made the decision to handle things on my own, from work projects and writing a book, to raising my children, managing a household and finances, and starting my own business.

That evening back in my hotel room, as I gave myself some time to think about the day, I realized I also didn't give others the chance to help me, even if they wanted to. When I set my mind on something, I decided how it should work, what the outcome should look like, and then do it by myself without deviation from the plan, regardless of my struggles along the way. At other times, my stubborn pride stopped me from accepting help from others "because it was my project and I could do it all by myself, because I'm strong and independent and this is my way to prove it."

As I reflected in my hotel room, I could see that over time I became overwhelmed by my to-do lists. I wondered why small, simple tasks seemed completely daunting. I often got to the point where I avoided new projects (unless they were things that seemed quick and easy, or were a form of procrastination) and abandoned old ones. Except, instead of fully giving up on the old projects to free up brain space for something new, I just moved them to the bottom of my to-do list. Many of my great ideas had been lost because I felt too overwhelmed to let them bloom. I regularly underestimated the amount of time it took to get a project done by myself. Possibly because a little project could be overshadowed by everything else I decided I needed to get done in a day. As a result, my to-do lists became ever longer—full of unfinished projects. By avoiding starting anything new or finishing anything hard, I avoided failure. At the extreme end of the spectrum, I would wake up some days feeling so overwhelmed with whatever I had on the go, including attending to my health and weight loss, that I completely avoided doing anything productive at all. Instead, I read, watched TV, played computer games, or even started a new fun project that kept me from thinking about the overwhelming ones already on the go, just to avoid my infinite to-do list. At the end of the day, I would feel even worse, because I felt guilty for not getting any of the things done I had planned that day, for being further behind, and for having less time to care for myself and my family. I felt like I'd wasted the day being too busy avoiding what needed to be done and had yet another reason to beat up on myself for not being good enough.

All of this rolled around in my head as I was trying to get a good night's sleep in my hotel room in anticipation of another day of learning about entrepreneurship. My sleep was troubled, at best. However, the next morning, I went back for the second day of the course and told Jay about my insights into all of my limiting beliefs about support and business that I had discovered the night before. Since Jay knew me well enough to be aware of many of my limiting beliefs, he fully agreed with me and congratulated me on my new awareness. When I told him I was going to write a book about the importance of asking for, accepting, and allowing support, he asked me whether this new project was going to end up being just something else on my to-do list. Initially taken aback, I felt defensive, until I realized the difference. I told him that the best way for me to learn something new is to teach it to someone else. My Personal Development Fairy Godfather laughed and told me to go for it. I left that course with the support to start this book.

After the entrepreneurship course, I continued to think more deeply about the importance of support, and I eventually understood the value of accepting support. I realized I would be able to complete tasks faster—and with more enthusiasm—if I accessed the resources and the people around me, whether it's hiring an expert in the task I'm tackling, or passing off household duties to my husband and kids. With support, I would be able to stay excited about a project, do a better job, and be proud of the end result. I would be much happier and wouldn't feel like I was going to fail. I wouldn't become so inundated with work that I felt forced to sacrifice quality time with my family. And I would have more time for myself to rejuvenate.

Like so many of us, I forget I can ask the people in my life for support and be confident they will help if I communicate my needs to them. My children will help me put the laundry away; my students will understand why their papers aren't marked if I explain that I only work a few days a week and have been at meetings or inundated with other tasks; and my friends and family will understand if I take some time to myself to be creative and write, rather than to visit. My husband is more than willing to help me when I ask him, because it means he gets a clean, clutter-free house, not to mention more of my time, in the long run.

The moral of the story? Having your belief system poked can lead to some incredible insights. When we stop, reflect, and pay attention, we find that people want to help each other. It builds a sense of connection and community, and makes us feel good to help others. **All you have to do is be willing to ask for and accept support.**

> *"We are each responsible for all of our experiences."*
> ∞ ***Louise Hay*** ∞

Why Don't We Ask for Support?

The course I took those many years ago provided me with the nudge I needed to change my life. I had ruled the Kingdom of I Can Do It All By Myself with such a tight reign for such a long time, and I knew changing my habits was not necessarily going to come easy. Most of all, I had no idea where to even start.

I now see so many people struggling with these same habits. I want to share with you the flaws I saw in my logic and the amazing approaches I learned for turning unsupportive thoughts and ideas into powerful strategies of support, all of which have made my life easier and much happier.

Once I decided I needed to change my attitude about support, the first thing I needed to do was figure out why I had such trouble asking for support in the first place. My answers revealed a lot about me.

Control: I don't want to ask for support because it takes too long to explain what I want done, and then I will have to go back and check that it is done right (a.k.a. my way).

Ego: No one else can possibly do it as well as me.

Meaning: If I allow someone to help me, it won't

mean as much and it won't be as much of an achievement.

Keeping agreements: I agreed to do it, so I'm going to do what I said I would.

Martyrdom: Can't you see how hard I work to get all these things done in a day? Where's my recognition? I do all this work, and no one appreciates me. In fact, no one loves me enough to help me or offer me support. I'll just keep struggling on my own. I'll get there eventually.

Burden: Everyone else is busy with their own stuff, and they don't have time for my requests. They won't be willing or able to help me anyways. It's not as important as whatever they're currently doing.

Fear of rejection: They won't want to help me. I'll feel rejected if I ask and they say "no." They can't help me with what I want to do. They won't understand what I'm trying to do. They might laugh at me if I tell them what I'm dreaming about or am actually doing.

Seeking approval: I'll show them I can do it all by myself and then they'll see what I'm capable of and that I am good enough.

And on and on it went. You wouldn't believe how much time I spent coming up with reasons for why I didn't ask for support. But what was I really doing? Keeping others out. I created situations where others couldn't help me, even if they wanted to, simply by wanting to have things done my way. By not asking for support and setting up my life in a way where others couldn't support me, or not letting others help me, I closed them out of my life. I avoided deep, meaningful relationships, and I prevented others from having these relationships with me.

It's taken close to ten years, but now I can say with confidence that I have made significant changes in my life. I see that the more I involve my husband in what I want and need, the more he's willing to help with cooking, cleaning, laundry, and looking after our children. And if I want some time to write or create, all I have to do is ask for what I want. I had to learn to trust him, though, before I would let him help me. I also chose to change the way I did things so he could help me, like creating a meal plan for the week, or changing my filing system so my husband could help file things away and not just add them to my pile to put away later.

I have also recognized the role my ego plays in my beliefs about being the only one who can do things the way they are "supposed" to be done. I have learned to trust that he—and others—can do things just as well as I can. I have learned I can make new choices when my ego tries to tell me I'm the only one who can do it. I have learned **I am loved and accepted for who I am, not for what I do.**

Once I took these difficult steps to actually ask for and accept support from others, everything started to change. It happened slowly at first, as we tested the waters, learned to trust each other, and became used to our new relationship. But change we did. The more willing I was to accept help, the happier we both became, and the easier it became to ask for support the next time, because I now knew what the results would be of asking and accepting assistance from others.

When I feel supported by my husband, our relationship becomes closer and stronger. We support each other. I have never felt as close to anyone as I do

Embracing Support

to him when we work together. Our happiness has increased tenfold since I decided I could trust him enough to allow him to help me.

Additional Reasons for Not Asking for or Accepting Support

As you can see from my example, there are many reasons why people don't ask for or accept support, and I've discovered these reasons are related to beliefs we have about ourselves and the world we live in. This list is by no means exhaustive. Do any of these perhaps apply to you?

- ∞ *Lack of knowledge*: This simply means these individuals have never learned what support is, what it can look like, the impact it can have on one's life, how to give or receive it, how to ask for it, and who to ask for what they want. Sometimes in a state of overwhelm, they forget they can ask for support, or just have no idea what support would be helpful to them, never mind who to ask.
- ∞ *Trust*: To accept support, individuals must trust the person from whom the support is coming, the type of support being offered, and that the support is unconditional (without a catch or hidden agenda). This means that if individuals don't trust others, they may not ask for support. Alternatively, if the type of support being offered is different from what the individual envisioned, they may not be open to any other form of support, or support from a person other than the one they thought the support *should* come from. Additionally, individuals may

have been taught to be wary of strangers, and the belief may exist that trusting others might create more problems than it solves and therefore it's better to keep to themselves.

∞ *Past rejection and disappointment/Feeling unworthy of support from others*: In past instances when individuals have asked for support from those who were unable or unwilling to support them, the individual asking may have felt pain and rejection, not realizing that in actuality, they weren't asking for the right kind of support or for support from the right person. However, this apparent rejection can create such hurt that the individual decides they are unworthy of support, are possibly even unloved or unlovable, and/or that their dream isn't worth dreaming in the first place, and they may give up on the dream altogether. All to avoid further pain.

∞ *Reciprocation and debt*: In these instances, individuals don't want to feel indebted to others or don't want to feel obligated to return the request for support and therefore don't ask for or accept support.

∞ *Avoidance*: Fear of failure, fear of success, and fear of project completion are big reasons individuals avoid asking for support. By not asking for or accepting support, individuals attempt to avoid completing projects or living their dreams because of the deep-rooted, subconscious belief of "I won't be able to do it anyway." These individuals stop asking for

Embracing Support

support or don't accept offered support because failure at an attempt would be even worse and more painful than never having tried. This fear is a major cause of lack of success and motivation in areas such as business and exercise. Individuals avoid the pain of failure by not starting, never considering the impact that support might have on being successful. They may even go so far as to create situations and drama in their lives and feel so overwhelmed with all they have committed themselves to that there is no room for even attempting to live their dreams. Instead of asking for support, they decide instead to avoid the work altogether by starting a new project, creating more drama, moving, searching for the "perfect" job or "perfect" relationship, watching TV, eating junk food, playing video games, drinking, smoking, doing drugs, or finding some other way of avoiding the task at hand.

∞ *Conscious choice*: These individuals may think they are just "too damn stubborn" (as my mother-in-law puts it) or that they actually do want to do things on their own. They're fully aware support is available, but choose not to access it in certain areas. Our conscious choices aren't always good choices, and I ask you to consider if choosing not to ask for support is truly in your best interest. On the other hand, consciously choosing to work on something independently can help you feel accountable and liberated, if you truly choose not to ask for support. These individuals may simply feel like they don't need support from others and they're managing quite well on their own.

I learned the importance of support the hard way: by going without it for so long that I became depressed, felt powerless, and was no longer excited about life. In sharing my stories, I hope to make this learning process easier for you than it was for me. As you can see by my examples in the previous pages, more than one of these categories may affect how much support we have or are willing to accept. I encourage you to think about your own reasons for not asking for or accepting support and write them in the space below. **Being aware of what's keeping you from having support is the first step to having more of it.**

I'd like you to begin by asking yourself, "What would life look like if I had more support every day?" Do you think you would be happier if you felt you were looked after more? If this is the case, you might want to also ask yourself, "Why don't I have it now?"

Now consider:

∞ What keeps you from asking for support?

_____
_____
_____
_____
_____
_____

Embracing Support

∞ If someone offers you support, how do you usually respond? (E.g. how do you respond to, "Do you want a hand carrying those items?")

_____
_____
_____
_____
_____

∞ Is there anyone from whom you accept support whenever they offer it? If yes, what makes it easy to accept their support?

_____
_____
_____
_____
_____

∞ Is there anyone from whom you rarely accept support even though they offer it? If yes, what makes it difficult to accept their support?

_____
_____
_____
_____
_____

Claudia R. Seiler-Mutton

> *"Every accomplishment starts with the decision to try."*
> ∞ **Gail Devers** ∞

Beware of Knights in Shining Armor

I am a supportive person by nature—sometimes too supportive. When people come to me with a problem or concern, I willingly, and sometimes unconsciously, pick up their torch and try to save their world. Like a knight in shining armor, I try to rescue them. I'm exaggerating a bit here, but not by much.

I've learned, though, that rescuing isn't the same as supporting. It doesn't work in the long term, and it's exhausting. As a rescuer, I can only do so much. Eventually, the individuals I'm rescuing have to make their own decisions and change their own circumstances. I can't do that for them. If they decide not to change, and the rescue cycle continues, I become exhausted. Eventually, I distance myself from that person, because I just can't "save them" anymore.

In turn, the individuals I was trying to support feel let down, resentful, and unsupported because I no longer come to their rescue. Typically, they go in search of a new knight in shining armor and create the same situation, except now they also complain about how the last knight let them down and abandoned them. The cycle can only end if they choose to rescue themselves, accept support for what it is, and enter into an equal, empowered, and supportive relationship, as a partner, not as a victim wanting to be rescued. Sound familiar? I've been on both sides of this equation, and

Embracing Support

neither one is very much fun. Because often enough, your knight in shining armor is just some idiot wrapped in tinfoil.

    I used to have a co-worker who always seemed to have something wrong: financial struggles, health concerns, family issues. If it wasn't one thing, it was something else. Her car was broken into; her boyfriend cheated on her; her apartment building had been condemned; she was in a car accident and hurt herself, and so on and so forth. Initially, I tried to help her however I could. We would talk and come up with various solutions to her problems. I tried to use my coaching skills to help her see a different perspective. I would even bring her flowers. Eventually, I realized no matter how hard I tried, she would always have a problem to overcome. It was her way to gain attention and feel loved. And I found myself starting to avoid her because I just didn't have the energy or time to listen to her grievances and rescue her anymore.
    That's when I realized the best way to truly support her was to empower her to become more accountable. She needed to take charge of her situation and her choices, not put the blame on others. The change in my support was gradual. When she told me about a tragedy in her life, I started asking her about the part she played in it, and how she planned on changing her circumstances. I asked her about the choices she had made up to that point and what new choices she could now make. I helped her find her own power again.
    Our relationship has changed significantly since I stopped trying to rescue her. These days, she tells me about her amazing new boyfriend, the money she won at the casino, and the condo she's going to buy. When

I stopped rescuing her, and started supporting her by guiding her to find her own power and happiness, we both felt better. Our relationship wasn't so heavy anymore. Now we visit as equals and friends without the expectation of results. This doesn't mean we don't help each other out. It just means we truly support each other, assisting, guiding, encouraging, empowering, and sometimes doing things for each other (as a favor), but never from the place of "I can't do it, you have to do it for me." Over time, I have witnessed an amazing transformation as this powerful woman has learned to claim her happiness by being accountable and empowered in her life.

On a side note, every so often, a knight in shining armor may be needed. An actual rescue might be necessary to bring people to the point where they can be independent. This may mean physically removing them from a dangerous situation or helping them out financially until they can get back on their feet. In the long term, however, **rescuing is not true support if it does not allow individuals to be accountable for their own actions and to be true to themselves**. Instead of potentially enabling the victim experience, teach them to become empowered and take control of their own situation. Tell the knight to hang up his tinfoil hat and grab a hammer instead. There's work to be done.

Good Fences Make Good Neighbors

When I feel supported, I feel strong. I feel clear on my goals and I get stuff done. When I have all the help, guidance, and champions I need, I feel like I can conquer the world. More than that, I feel like I have the power within me to accomplish all of this, and still be true to—and take care of—myself. It means it's okay for me to set boundaries on what I will and will not do for others and how I'm willing to spend my time, without feeling like I'm letting others down or feeling guilty for turning someone away. I can also set boundaries on what I'm willing to accept from others. Setting clear boundaries can be the most important thing you can do to support yourself and others.

Think back to our poor overwhelmed princess, whose yard was overrun with the neighbor's sheep who wouldn't stay on their own side of the fence. She was so busy dealing with the chaos that ensued—being pulled in too many directions, with too many expectations on her time—to focus on her priorities. **When we don't set clear boundaries (or have strong fences), we may let others take advantage of us and our time without even realizing it.** Setting boundaries means you are clear on what you are willing and not willing to do to support others and how much time you are willing to spend supporting them, as well as yourself. This is where you put your foot down and say "No more!" Clear boundaries mean a clear answer to the question: "How much am I willing to give of myself?" The old saying "good fences make good neighbors" came about for a reason.

Meanwhile, Back at the Kingdom

In 2007, disaster struck the Kingdom of I Can Do It All By Myself. The Queen was diagnosed with cancer and, after the surgery to remove the tumor, she had a stroke. *The morning after her surgery, the Queen could not see and she could not move her limbs. Over time and with rehabilitation (and sheer determination), the Queen regained much of her independence and was eventually able to go home. However, because of the stroke, she had lost some of her mobility and reflexes and a large portion of her vision, which meant she couldn't drive any more. Being the elder child and a nurse, the Princess felt she was pressured by the medical team and the Queen to take on much of the responsibility of caring for the Queen during her initial five-month rehabilitation and recovery. She was even asked to take the Queen to the Princess' castle and care for her there.*

However, the Princess had two little princesses of her own to look after: a three-year-old and a brand new three-week-old baby. There was no room in the little castle for the Queen, so she stayed in the hospital until she was able to go to a specialized rehabilitation facility. In the meantime, the Queen was transferred several times to different hospitals due to a bed shortage, and each time the Queen expected the Princess to go along to assist the Queen with the transfer. The weight of looking after the Queen and taking her to various appointments and accompanying her through her rehabilitation laid heavily on the Princess' shoulders, alongside all of her other responsibilities.

By the time the littlest princess was six months old, she had accompanied the Princess and the Queen to every one of the five hospitals in the

Embracing Support

Kingdom, as well as a few in a neighboring kingdom, supporting the Queen through her rehabilitation. Once the Queen's condition improved enough and she was more mobile, she urged the Princess to take her to her farm home in the country on weekend passes. The Princess, wanting to help the Queen get out of the hospitals and improve her mental state by being at home, eventually agreed. Often the Princess had both of her children on those weekends as well. Sometimes she felt like she was taking care of three little ones, with one being much more demanding than the others. Because the Queen had lost so much of her independence, she would get frustrated with herself and with the Princess when she wasn't able to do what she wanted, when she wanted. It was difficult for the Queen to be dependent on others for so many of her needs.

Often, by the time the Princess and her three charges arrived at the farm on a Friday night, the baby needed to be changed and fed, and supper needed to be started for the Queen and the other little princess. The Princess often resented her additional responsibilities and felt she was missing out on precious time with her new baby. After all, she didn't ask for this responsibility. She felt it was expected of her.

Eventually the Princess realized she wasn't supporting the Queen anymore. She was trying to rescue her. Being her rescuer, she begrudgingly said "yes" to all the Queen's demands. Because she was a medical professional, and because she was on maternity leave from ruling other parts of the kingdom, it was assumed that the Princess had some flexibility with her time, while the Princess' younger sister didn't have a vehicle, worked full time, and had various other responsibilities and commitments.

Looking back, the Princess realized she could have reinforced the fences around her kingdom and said: "I can't . . ." "I'm not willing to . . ." or "I'm not able to . . ." She could have insisted her sister come along and help out. She could have asked the Prince to take their older daughter to his parents' place on the weekend, or she could have asked friends to help the Queen. Instead, she didn't say anything. She felt guilty saying "no" and making herself and her children the priority, because, after all, she was the Princess of The Kingdom of I Can Do It All by Myself.

I know today that, if I had told Mom I was getting burnt out and wanted her to ask one of her friends to take her on a day trip, she would have understood. She could see my behavior, she knew what I was feeling, and she hated asking me for help because I always did it so grudgingly. Our relationship suffered greatly because neither of us conceded what the other truly needed.

If we had stopped at any point throughout the madness and said to each other and to the health care professionals involved, "We can't do this anymore, we need help," a different solution would have been found. By stopping the struggle and asking for support, I would have significantly changed the outcome of our relationship.

As much as I wanted to help Mom, I just couldn't

support her the way she needed me to. I was neglecting myself and my children and our mother-daughter relationship had turned into a nurse-client relationship—with really poor pay. Mom felt the tension too, which led her to feel victimized rather than supported.

Helping her didn't turn into true support until we finally sat down and set some boundaries. We had a conversation about how I was able to help her, what I was willing to do, and how much time I was willing (not able, but willing) to spend. Mom also set stipulations. Together we discussed how a weekend at the farm could be more productive, and how Mom could regain her independence by either doing more for herself or by having me do things with her—not for her.

We also agreed she could ask her friends and my sister for help. Before long, I was able to start taking care of myself again. We both recognized I wouldn't be able to take care of her at all if I didn't start caring for myself. We both benefitted from setting boundaries. We were able to restore our mother-daughter relationship, and she felt motivated to become stronger and more independent. Five months after her stroke and rehab in a specialized facility, Mom was on a plane to Switzerland and helped her own ailing mother clean house and prepare for a move to an alternate level of care facility. I know exactly where I get my stubbornness from.

Setting boundaries is about taking charge and making agreements. Boundaries are an important part of a supportive relationship, and they can go both ways. You may find yourself in a situation where you need to set boundaries about how much and what type of support you give to others, but also about what and how much you're willing to accept from someone else.

After my first daughter was born, my mom and I talked about how much of her support I was willing to accept in looking after my first baby. We had some very different views on caring for a newborn, and I wanted to be clear that, as well-meaning as she might be, certain types of stories and advice were neither needed nor appreciated. It took some time, but I was eventually able to clearly articulate my beliefs about parenting and support, especially when it came to my children. For example, I had to remind my mom that her telling me stories of children suffering in other parts of the world were not reassuring me on my ability to protect my children. Although it took some doing, once I was able to clearly express what I wanted, we could enjoy each other's company without either of us feeling any strain in the relationship.

Now is a great time to think about establishing boundaries with people in your life. I believe we all have the best of intentions in wanting to support each other. I also believe the greatest love and support we can give each other is to be clear on what we want and what we need support to look like. Setting boundaries is the first step in establishing the kind of support you want from others.

Have you ever found yourself in a situation that started out as a willingness to help someone, which then evolved into being taken for granted and not being able to say "no" until you just weren't able to do it anymore? If you have, I encourage you to think about whether or not this type of rescuing truly helps you or the person you're trying to support. If you're in this type of relationship now, perhaps it's time to sit down and have a conversation and set those boundaries. How do you think your relationship could be improved by building a better fence? What are you willing to keep doing in this relationship, and what needs to change? Please take a few minutes to reflect on this now before continuing on.

How Does Support Translate into Everyday Life?

In order to feel more empowered by having more support, you first need to know what kind of support you want and need. If you are a person who has used a support network effectively in the past, you may know exactly what support looks like for you. On the other hand, if you have had very little support in the past, or if you aren't aware that support is available, you may find it more challenging to clearly articulate what you want or need.

One of my biggest challenges has always been to identify how I need others to support me. Because I've always been so self-reliant, my instinct has been to do it all by myself. When someone asked me, "How can I support you?" or "What can I do to help?" I never knew what to say, because I didn't know what the possibilities were. In other words, I didn't know what support looked like. It's kind of like describing the vastness of the ocean to someone who has never even seen a picture of it. How can we imagine something we have no concept of? So let's take some time to build a new perspective of what support might look like in your life.

I've been carrying an extra fifteen pounds since the summer before I started nursing school. After I had my babies, those fifteen pounds invited some friends and relatives over and now I'm a good thirty pounds heavier than I was when I graduated from high school. I'm in denial about the implications of my weight gain and say things like, "Oh, thirty pounds isn't so bad," or "At 5'7" I still look pretty good." The fact is, though, I'm not happy about it, and every day when I look in the mirror, I have that nasty little self-talk about this extra weight and all the things it's keeping me from accomplishing.

I've been trying to lose this weight for as long as I can remember. I have tried going to the gym; I swim regularly; I pay attention to my diet; and I try to get enough sleep. But no matter how hard I try, I can't stick with it for any length of time. Even though I've had some success and have even lost as much as ten pounds at a time, I can't sustain any success on my own, and I just give up. Whatever weight I've lost finds me again—and usually quite quickly.

This is where support makes all the difference. I have enough motivation to get started, but because I've only ever tried to lose weight on my own, I have no idea what effective support might look like. I don't even know where to start looking for that kind of support. What's a princess to do?

Role Models

If you're having trouble figuring out what support looks like, you can look at the support that others in similar situations are benefiting from. For weight-loss role models, for example, I first thought about Oprah or Kirstie Alley—two famous personalities who have struggled with their weight over the years. I asked myself, "What kind of support did these two ladies have to help them lose weight?" I remembered hearing about specialized kitchens, personal chefs and trainers, and so on. The list is long and involves a lot of money. Well, I have neither the time nor the money for that kind of weight-loss program. Does this mean I am doomed to forever carry these extra pounds? Of course not. What works for one person does not necessarily work for another. So, back to the drawing board to find the right kind of support.

My friend's experience provides a more realistic model of support. Support for her weight loss came in the form of a support group, as well as regular appointments with a trainer at the gym, friends and family who encouraged her along the way, some cooking classes to help her change the way she shopped for and prepared her meals, and a close friend she could call on any time she felt like she was struggling or falling off her wagon. Was it an easy process? No way. But because of her support network, she had the power and the motivation to keep moving toward her goal. I'm so pleased to tell you she has had phenomenal success. To use her words, she has "released" 85 pounds and looks absolutely fantastic. My sister is doing much of the same and, with the help of her support group, has lost over 100 pounds (in just under a year) by being a part of an ongoing weight loss support system. Support works.

Now that I'm finally ready to commit myself to

success and embark on this journey of releasing weight, I know I'm going to take a few pages out of their books and adapt some of their strategies. I also know that when I've joined a group or a class at the gym in the past, it's been much easier to make the commitment to regularly go for a workout. But by looking at what others are doing, and what is working for them, I can start to conceptualize or visualize the types of support I could ask for. If I'm clear about what I want, I'll figure out what I need to do and what support to ask for, and then I can find the right approach for me. Or better yet, I'll ask someone for support to help me figure out what the options are in order to find what the right approach might be for me.

Getting the Right Kind of Support

Once you know what different types of support could look like, you need to choose the option that works best for you and communicate that clearly to your support network. This may sound simple, but could take some practice—especially if you're used to ruling a kingdom all by yourself.

By the time my girls were six and nine years old, my husband and I both worked full time, and although my mom was doing much better and was much more independent, I was still my mom's primary caregiver. I helped her with home maintenance, and drove her to appointments, the grocery store, and other destinations when her friends were not able to support her with transportation. My husband and I had a house with a yard in the city, plus my mom's farm property to look

Embracing Support

after. Life was busy, and 24 hours in a day just wasn't enough. By the time I got home from work and put supper on the table, I didn't have much time to clean up. So, when I would walk in the door, I'd dump whatever I was carrying with me—bills, work stuff, student papers, whatever—on the big kitchen counter, where there was lots of space. Eventually this pile would make its way to my office table, and pretty soon I had a huge mound of paper to wade through. Honestly, this endless paper trail was the bane of my existence.

For the most part, I'd gotten used to the clutter and had learned to tune it out, but my husband hated it. For him, the pile of paper in the office was a huge source of stress because he couldn't help me with it. The crazy thing is, in some ways, my clutter made me feel in control because I'm the only one who could do anything about it. It's *my* clutter. I had effectively created a situation my husband couldn't help me with even if I wanted him to.

The part that bugged me was it was stressing him out, and that it had an effect on my kids' health and happiness. Plus, I'd get frustrated when I just didn't have the time to get to it because I have beliefs about what a neat house should look like, and how to keep a marriage happy.

My husband tried to support me with this constant clutter turmoil. His version of support, however, usually involved me being bombarded with questions when I was preoccupied with something else: "Do we still need this?" "Can I get rid of this?" Or he would go through the pile on the counter and throw out things he thought were no longer needed. Nothing important ever got thrown out, but sometimes things I wanted to keep for some reason or another were tossed, which drove me up the wall. I know he was trying to help, but it just made things worse. That, to me, was not supportive. It actually just frustrated me more and left me feeling pressured, more stressed, hurt, or neglected. Clearly, this was not the right kind of support for me.

I did feel supported when he would get the kids out of my hair for half an hour or so, did homework with them, went for a walk or played with them in the basement, or started supper. It meant I could spend a focused few minutes on organizing the mess. If I set ten undisturbed minutes aside for focused work, amazing things happen. That, to me, is support from my husband. Unfortunately he can't read minds, so I needed to ask him for what I wanted, which is a big part of having enough support. When I'm clear on what I need and ask for it, we're both happy.

In general, I've learned if I want to have enough support—the kind that truly is supportive—I need be very clear on what I need, and what that support should look like. Only then can I figure out who will be the best person to give me that support.

Now it's time to think about what support might look like for you. The following series of questions is designed to help you come up with your own definition of support. Feel free to use my definition of support as a starting point: **a way to empower individuals to use the strength and love from others to create something miraculous for themselves.** Ask yourself, "What kind of support do I need in order to create that happiness and empowerment for myself in any of my life areas?" (Yes, you do have the right and

Embracing Support

the power to feel happy and empowered.)

If you're having trouble visualizing this for yourself, remember to think about the ideas presented in the role model section above, and don't worry if you can't answer all of these questions yet. Do your best and remember you can always return to this activity once you have more information. You can also access a downloadable PDF booklet containing all of the exercises throughout this book on my website: www.healwithsupport.com/resources. Being clear about support can be challenging. At this point it's most important to be honest with yourself.

Activity: A Personal View of Support

∞ Think of a situation in which you felt truly supported by others, or where you observed someone else receive good support. Write down what was happening at that point in your life (or theirs) that made it feel like true support.

_____
_____
_____
_____
_____
_____
_____

∞ What is your life like, or what could your life be like when you feel supported? What are you able to do, and who are you able to be, when you feel supported?

∞ When you are truly supported, what do you feel?

∞ What could the people in your life do to make you feel more supported (stronger, more powerful, like you're living your life's purpose, etc.)?

∞ What do you do now, or what could you do now, to support yourself and create that feeling of support?

Embracing Support

_____
_____
_____
_____
_____
_____
_____

- ∞ Guided by your answers to these questions, write your own definition of support. What does support mean to you?

_____
_____
_____
_____
_____
_____
_____

If you're finding it challenging to answer some of these questions, it may simply be that you're having difficulty imagining all the possibilities of what support could look like because you may not have had an experience of what is available to you. Remember that anything is possible. Find a role model who has the ideal version of the life you want—strong, happy, and empowered with support from others—and follow their example. Ask yourself, what is it about that person that makes you think they are powerful and living their life's purpose; that they are loved and supported? In *Awaken the Giant Within: How to Take Immediate Control of Your Mental, Emotional, Physical and Financial Destiny*, Anthony Robbins encourages us to look to the successes of others to create our own dreams. Bottom line: Someone, somewhere out there is doing what you want to accomplish. Follow in their footsteps to get there yourself. One step at a time.

Dream Big

I once had a conversation with a close friend who told me he wanted a good job with a "decent income" and "reasonable pay." I asked him what he considered "decent" and "reasonable." When he answered "a minimum of $20/hour," I asked him what kept him from thinking bigger in regards to the value of his time. By his own admission, he wasn't even aware he had limited what he thought was achievable and realistic, and what his time was worth. He realized his own beliefs about his skills and abilities were limiting him from achieving more. Then he said it was time to "start living in a bigger box," meaning that it was time to start dreaming bigger.

This is true for support as well. If we have never experienced what it feels like, or if we don't know what life could be like with support, we'll keep living in the same-sized box, never questioning why we don't have more—more support, more money, more love, more friends, more fun, and so on.

I believe we learn to dream as children, but we often forget how to dream big right about the time we graduate from high school. The real world sets in, and we see ourselves limited by what society deems to be the standard for our age, educational level, socioeconomic class, and cultural background. We let the opinions of others affect our beliefs about what is possible. I also believe this to be the case with support—how much we have and what we ask for and accept from others.

Yet, when it comes to dreaming big and making our dreams come true, this is where support becomes important. Having support can mean the difference between success and failure. Having support means having someone to lean on when you need a little extra help. Having support can help you to become a greater, grander version of yourself. Having support can mean you're willing to make changes, such as a applying for a new job, going back to school, taking a chance on a relationship, or starting your own business. **Having support can help you move past your fears and allow you to start dreaming again.** Having support can help us dream bigger, can make the difference between just dreaming and turning those dreams into reality. Having support means you have someone who believes in you, who infuses you with confidence and hope that your dreams are possible, and who empowers you towards happiness.

"When you open your mind to the impossible, you might discover the truth."
∞ ***Walter Bishop*** ∞
Fringe (Television Series)

A Few Last Points about Being Clear

Before you put your new knowledge into practice, I'd like to spend a bit more time on clearly identifying exactly what you want and need in terms of support. Clearly articulating your needs can be challenging, and will take some practice. Here is a tool I've had a lot of success with, called a Contrast List.

In his book *Law of Attraction: The Science of Attracting More of What You Want and Less of What You Don't*, Michael J. Losier uses the Contrast List to show how we can attract exactly what we do want, by first understanding what we don't want. He suggests creating a list of everything that is currently not working in your life, and then writing the contrasting ideal on the opposite side of the page. Here is a short excerpt from my Contrast List. As you read through it, take note of any items that are relevant to your situation. Also, notice how many of my difficulties were related to not having enough support and to my limiting beliefs.

I Don't Want...	Therefore I Do Want...
– To feel alone and unsupported because I'm living my life based on someone else's limiting beliefs about what I can and can't do	– To receive genuine support from someone who believes in the same things as I do and can talk me through my self-doubt (I want empowerment) – To live my life based on my own dreams and goals, with support
– To work so many hours that I do not have enough time for my family (especially my kids) and friends – To feel a lack of:	– To only work three days/week, so I have more time to spend with my kids and for myself – To feel my purpose in life has nothing to do

Embracing Support

- Time - Money - Energy - Peace - Love - Freedom	with the number of hours I spend at work - To easily manifest goals in my new business and to have a consistent income, or more than I need to cover my bills with extra at month end - To learn about and feel more abundance
- To feel that my contributions at work aren't valued and that I'm taken for granted	- To contribute valuable and sought-after services - To feel valued and to be recognized for my contributions
- To feel unclear about my life's purpose and direction or incapable of doing something important (like writing or starting my own business) because of limiting beliefs	- To feel powerful and capable within my own beliefs, regardless of those around me - To feel confident and focused in my goals and dreams and steadily move towards them - To have a clear vision and mission and move towards them easily and generate innumerable results
- To feel like my husband and I don't have any quality time together because we're too busy	- To feel like we have quality time in our relationship, every time we spend time together, regardless of where we are

- To feel tired and overwhelmed with the amount of work I have to do at work and at home	- To feel calm, peaceful, and able to enjoy my life, my family, and my job (in short, to have balance) - To have time to myself where I can focus on what needs to be done and get it done quickly without interruptions

- To feel alone and unsupported in:
   o Taking care of my kids
   o Losing weight
   o Moving to a new house
   o Getting a job
	- To feel like I can trust others with my requests for help without fear of rejection
	- To feel like I can call on a number of people on short notice, if need be, who would be able to help me with my burdens
	- To have someone to watch my kids so I can go out for a few hours
	- To have fun moving my body, releasing weight, and planning meals with someone
	- To have someone to talk to about my feelings

- To feel like I have to do it all on my own	- To trust in others and believe that they can and will support me - To know there are people I can call on for support

Activity: My Contrast List

Now it's your turn. Develop your own Contrast List. The more specific you are, the better. Complete the "I Don't Want" column first, and then write the opposite into the "I Do Want" column. The clearer you are about what you do want, the easier it will be to ask for the support you need.

I Don't Want . . .	Therefore I Do Want . . .

(Note: if you'd like a blank copy of this chart, go to my website www.healwithsupport.com/resources.)

If you're struggling with this activity, make a list of everything you're not happy about instead, and then write the opposite on the other side of the page. This may help clarify what you do want. Remember also to ask for support if you're stuck figuring out what the opposite might be, and remember to look at your role models. Once you're clear on what you want to create in your life, you can start looking at the support you might need to help you get there.

So, What Have We Learned?
In this chapter:
- ✓ We've defined support as a way to empower individuals to use the strength and love from others to create something miraculous for themselves and started creating your own definition of support.
- ✓ We've outlined reasons why individuals might not ask for or accept support.
- ✓ We've detailed what support could look like and how you can broaden your perspective on what support can be.
- ✓ We've looked at how "supporting" is different from "rescuing."
- ✓ We've discussed the importance of boundaries and identifying role models.
- ✓ We've started looking at how to get the right kind of support.
- ✓ We've created a Contrast List of what's not working in our lives and have started focusing on what we do want.
- ✓ We've had a glimpse of what a happy life with support could look like.

Embracing Support

Whew! That was a lot to get through. I hope you're still with me, and I hope you've given yourself the gift of reflecting on all of this information. When you're ready, now that you have a basic understanding of what support is and what might prevent you from having it, it's time to focus on getting clear on what type of support would help the most, and how to get it from the right people.

> *"You attract to your life whatever you give your attention, energy, and focus to, whether wanted or unwanted."*
> ∞ *Michael J. Losier* ∞

Strategy 2: Get Clear on What You Want (Accepting Support)

"Everything you'll ever need to know is within you; the secrets of the universe are imprinted on the cells of your body."
∞ *Dan Millman* ∞

As you may have discovered, understanding what support you already have access to and how to set limits is an important first step in getting exactly the support that will help you the most. Now let's look at getting exactly what you need in a clear and clean way.

Why Don't I Have What I Want?

In *How to Get from Where You Are to Where You Want to Be: The 25 Principles of Success*, Jack Canfield writes, "One of the main reasons why people don't get what they want is they haven't decided what they want." He goes on to explain that this tendency is rooted in our childhood. As babies, we know exactly what we want and we cry when we don't get it. But as we get older, we are often taught there are limits to what we can have or should want, based on the beliefs of others, and we adopt these beliefs as our own. Over time, we forget what we really want, and start behaving the way others expect us to, wanting what we think they want us to want.

When I read Canfield's book, I couldn't help but think of my youngest daughter when she was five. When she didn't like something, she had a full-out temper tantrum, or at least a hissy-fit. As her parent, I swooped onto the scene trying to teach her proper behavior and that temper tantrums are not appropriate. It hit me one day that I was suppressing her individuality and her free will by teaching her "how" to behave. So, I decided to change the way I responded to her tantrums.

We started to talk about how she could choose a different behavior to get what she really wanted, and we worked on her using her words. This gave her more control over the situation, plus she learned how to use her words to ask for what she really wanted. It didn't mean she always got it, but I was much more lenient when she asked for what she wanted instead of having a fit because she didn't get what she wanted. Even now that she's almost a teenager, when I disagree with what she wants, or feel it isn't something she needs, I explain to her exactly why I don't want her to have that or why I won't let her have what she's after. Sometimes it actually works.

Reclaim Your Power

In his book, Canfield also states that we need to be clear on what we want out of life if we want to "re-own" our power. This philosophy applies to support as well. Canfield explains that we give away our power when we say things like, "I don't know. I don't care. It doesn't matter to me. Whatever." When we accept support that is unsolicited or support that is not what we really want or need, simply because it's offered or because we don't want to hurt the other person's feelings by refusing, we also give away our power.

Canfield provides an alternative approach: "When you are confronted with a choice, no matter how small or insignificant, act as if you have a preference. Ask yourself, 'If I did know, what would it be? If I did care, what would I prefer? If it did matter, what would I rather do?'" He explains that not making decisions is a habit that is easily broken by doing the opposite: making decisions—regardless of how small—thus reclaiming your power. The Contrast List you developed for yourself is a perfect example of this theory in action.

If you give your power away and accept support that isn't what you need simply because it's offered, what you receive is no longer support. Instead you are giving away your power to a potential rescuer. **If you are clear on the support you want, you can ask for it precisely** or refuse support if it's not what you want or if it's not supportive. In this way, when support comes your way, you will know exactly what to accept from others and what to refuse.

∞ ∞ ∞

I've been a nurse for about 25 years now, but it is only recently that I realized I never wanted to be one—it was my mother's dream for me. I always wanted to write and create—to be a writer or a singer. Because both my parents feared for my financial independence, they'd say things like: "You can't make money doing that." "It's difficult to be successful in the music business." "Running a business is hard work." "Get an education and a real job so you can make money to support your dreams." (Thankfully, the one thing they never insisted on was for me to get a haircut.)

Based on their fears and beliefs about life being difficult and that only the hard-working get rich, I decided I should want what they want. I stopped dreaming about singing and writing. I stopped being true to myself. I did what they wanted, but I was miserable and depressed going through nursing school and for many years thereafter because I was denying who I really was.

I also adopted my mom's beliefs about asking for support. My mom prized independence above all else and that belief became deeply ingrained in me. I believed that in order to be strong and independent I should not ask for support because that would be a sign of weakness. Instead, I should be proud to be independent, and not rely on anyone. I took on my mom's belief that I had to do it on my own in order for accomplishments to be meaningful. It wouldn't be nearly as much of an achievement if I had asked for support along the way.

Essentially, I was living my mom's dreams and beliefs, and I refused support from anyone who was willing to support me. I had to do it my way, the hard way. Over time, I alienated my closest friends and best support systems. Instead, I found myself surrounded by people whom I could support, who constantly needed me to bail them out of a situation, because I was the strong and independent one. I had no one left to ask for support.

This worked for a while when I was on my own—the lone wolf, the rebel in leather on my motorcycle, not needing anyone or anything. Wasn't I the one to be envied? But once I had a husband and kids, maintaining my standard of independence meant becoming Supermom. I had an almost full-time job, a family, a house, and an ailing parent to look after. Is it any wonder I was getting burned out? But did I ask for help? No. I had to do it by myself. And then I wondered why my emotions were a mess, my relationships with my mom and my husband were suffering, I rarely spent quality time with my kids, I had very few friends I still kept in touch with, I was gaining weight, and I was tired all the time.

If any of this sounds familiar, I'm happy to tell you that all of this changed—almost immediately—the minute I started asking for and accepting support from those who loved me the most. Once I started trusting my husband to help me, and I finally let him help, we had more time to do things together. All of the day-to-day responsibilities were completed that much faster, I wasn't overwhelmed anymore, he felt more in control, connected, and purposeful because we worked together, and our relationship is closer now than it has been in the past fifteen years. Simply because I started asking for and accepting support.

How did I finally learn to release my mother's beliefs about independence and seek out support? It started when a friend of mine invited me to hear Michael Losier speak. I was inspired by his message, bought his *Law of Attraction* book, and actually read it. I took his advice and started making a list of what I didn't want. It was a long one.

Once I wrote my Contrast List, I felt like some of the pressure was off. There it was in black and white. All of the pressure caused by limiting thoughts and resistance to what was going on in my life was finally out of my head and on paper. My energy levels changed because I didn't have to carry that burden anymore. With those thoughts in front of me, I could now let some of them go and begin translating my "I Don't Wants" into "I Do Wants."

I had trouble at first, so I started thinking about people I knew who seemed to be in ideal relationships and living ideal lives. I went through a process similar to a set of questions I'll ask you to complete in an upcoming section. I moved from a focus on what I didn't want to what I did want. Once I had a clear idea of the direction I wanted to go, I started putting a plan of action into place to help me get there. The interesting thing is, as soon as I stopped fighting against what I didn't want and started to focus on and allow what I did want, my subconscious mind started finding a way for me to have all of those things. I realize now just how many of the things on the "I Do Want" side my Contrast List I now have. By being clear on what I wanted, I cleared a path to attract these new situations to come into my life, and many of them did, without any conscious effort on my part. That seemingly simple list really is an amazing tool.

Ask the Right Person (The Right Way and at the Right Time)

If you've worked through the Contrast List and the questions I asked as part of the previous chapter, you've hopefully developed your own definition of support. Now it's simply a matter of asking for that support, right? While there's definitely some truth to that, I have also learned it is important to ask the right person in the right way and at the right time. Let's take a bit of time to clarify exactly what you're asking for, so you can choose the right person to ask for what you want.

Think about: Who do you ask for support? Are these individuals truly the best people to ask for what you need, or are you simply asking them because they are there? Or perhaps you're asking them because you feel like they *should* be able to support you?

The Right Person

One of the mistakes I consistently made was expecting and asking my husband for support with certain aspects of housekeeping and childcare. I had a belief that we should equally split home and childcare responsibilities. In reality, our responsibilities were split fairly evenly, but I also needed to acknowledge my husband possesses gifts and talents that make him better at certain things, like freely playing with our girls and enforcing discipline, while I possess gifts and talents that make me better at getting us organized and functioning smoothly as a cohesive and loving family unit.

Together we make an amazing team and have established the roles we play in our relationship through mutual consent. However, I've learned to simply not ask him to do certain things, especially if I want them done my way. As much as he wants to support me, there are some tasks he simply isn't capable of (or I'm better at), and asking him to do those things will never give me what I want, no matter how much he loves me and tries. For example, I never ask him to tidy my office, clean the bathrooms, go grocery shopping (except maybe for milk), or make sure the girls are dressed appropriately for school. Those just aren't his strengths. On the other hand, if I ask him to change the oil in my motorbike or work in the yard, I am playing to his strengths. These are tasks he excels at and enjoys doing. It's not that I can't do these things myself, I just prefer not to. Likewise, he knows not to ask me for certain things. Other people are more suited to help. But he forgets sometimes, and when he complains about me not mowing the grass or shoveling snow, I say, "Sure, I'll get right on that. Will you be scrubbing the toilets in the meantime?"

I've also discovered that if I can let go of some of my controlling (or perhaps perfectionist) attitudes on how I want the laundry folded and put away, or what I want the girls to wear, and can accept it might not look the way I want it to, then I can ask him for support in those areas. Often the tasks get completed faster and I can focus on other things. **When the type of support really does matter, I ask for exactly what I want** and perhaps even give very clear directions. Through experience, I have learned what support I can ask him for, and what support is best asked of someone else. Likewise, if you are clear on what you need, you can ask the right person, and get exactly the type of support you ask for.

Activity: Getting Clear About Support
- ∞ Think about one area of your life (physical, intellectual/mental, emotional, spiritual, financial/occupational, environmental, or social) in which you could benefit from more support. What support from others would help

you create change in this life area?

_____
_____
_____
_____
_____
_____

∞ If anything were possible, what would you really want from others?

_____
_____
_____
_____
_____
_____

∞ Think about the people you usually ask for support. Who are your biggest sources of support? Write their names in the column on the left.

_____	_____
_____	_____
_____	_____
_____	_____
_____	_____
_____	_____
_____	_____

∞ Take a minute to think about the names on your list. Do you choose certain people for certain types of support? Or do you always ask the same person no matter the situation? For example, would you ask the same people to babysit your kids as you would to mow your lawn when you're on holidays? Who would you call in case of an emergency?

∞ In the right-hand column above, write the corresponding type(s) of support you could ask for—but are not currently asking for—from each of the people listed in the left-hand column. This could be time, money, a ride, babysitting, or a new job—whatever comes to mind. Think big.

Consider the names and tasks in your list carefully. Ask yourself if your responses are based on what they really are willing or able to support you with, or if you are attaching judgments and limitations to whether or not each person could truly support you in a meaningful way. Sometimes we make assumptions or are too scared to ask for what we really want, and don't ask or even consider that individual for what might turn out to be the best support of all. Please take a few minutes to reflect on this. It will become very relevant when we move on to looking at how your beliefs affect the amount of support you have.

Also think about this question: do you usually get the support you ask for, or are your requests often denied? The answer will tell you about the beliefs you may have about support. If you usually get what you ask for, you are more likely to ask again in the same manner. If you sometimes feel disappointed because you don't get the support you need, you're less likely to ask for help again, at least not from that person. However, if you feel like there's no one to help, you may also feel like there's no use in asking. All of these points play into our beliefs about support. The more you believe support is available, and that it's the perfect support for your needs, the more likely you are to consistently ask for support. If, however, you believe you are alone, that you do not have anyone in your life who will or can support you, you will be less likely to find the support you need.

Remember, in addition to asking, you also need to believe support is available to you and be open to accepting it when it comes your way. I can't tell you how many times I've heard people say, "There is no one to support me," when in truth these individuals simply weren't asking the right people, or weren't willing to accept support from those who did offer it.

I strongly encourage you to start thinking about and becoming aware of the beliefs you have regarding the support you currently have in your life. You'll see this more clearly in upcoming chapters as we examine the role beliefs have in support. For now, start listening to your inner voice and become aware of your thoughts, especially the ones that tell you "no," "can't," "unable," "not deserving," and so on. Louise Hay teaches that **"every thought we think is creating our future."** Therefore, being aware of these inner dialogues can help you reduce their power over your other thoughts and behaviors, by purposely changing the language you use to more supportive thoughts like

Embracing Support

"can," "will," "able," "deserving," and so on.

Right Person, Wrong Support

On occasion you may ask the right people for specific types of support but find the results lacking. Even though they are able to support you, the support provided is not what you want or asked for. You get their version of what they think you want or what they think would support you the best.

At this point you have three choices:
- ∞ You can accept their version of the support and make the most of it without feeling angry, hurt, disappointed, resentful, or full of self-doubt because you didn't get exactly what you asked for.
- ∞ You can discuss with them what you are truly asking for and ask if they are willing to support you in this.
- ∞ You can stop asking them for support because they may not be the right person for what you truly want and need.

When you find yourself in this situation, you can choose to accept the support as well-meaning, intended to help you, or you can choose not to accept the support. Either way, you need to proceed objectively, without reading any anger, resentment, or blame into the situation. If the support wasn't what you asked for, please don't assume the "mistakes" were made on purpose. **You can choose how you react to what other people say and do**, and you can *choose* not to let their thoughts, feelings, and actions affect you. What someone else may perceive as extremely helpful for you may, in fact, appear to you as undermining, derogatory, ignorant, or simply disrespectful.

In truth, their actions may have nothing to do with you at all, but rather with their beliefs about how to best provide support. Parents often fit into this category, as we try to do what we think is best for our children. It doesn't mean it's right, but often it's well-meaning. In the end, though, each of us can choose how we react to the situation and what we read into it.

Meanwhile, Back at the Kingdom

The birth of the Princess' first baby was difficult and severely aggravated a previous back injury. She wasn't able to move around very well for the first three months of motherhood and had a tough time with all sorts of things. The Queen wanted to help the Princess by providing the best care possible for her brand-new baby girl. The Queen was so excited about her first grandchild, who happened to be born the day after the Queen's birthday. She offered to cook for the Princess, clean the castle, and do laundry, as her mother had done for her. She was trying to be a helpful grandparent, as is often a custom—and sometimes even an expectation—in many cultures.

However, the Princess' perception of the Queen's support was a different matter. She second-guessed her own abilities as a new mom and felt she wasn't good enough in the Queen's eyes. Instead of accepting the support from the Queen, the Princess felt judged and tremendously overwhelmed by feeling like she had to do it all by herself. The Princess thought the Queen was helping because she believed her own daughter was incapable.

If the Princess had been aware of her own beliefs and able to deal with her feelings of inadequacy at being a novice parent, she could have accepted the Queen's help for what it was meant to be: support for a new parent offered out of love. Instead, the Princess thought the Queen was purposely trying to teach her how to be a good parent, which was the last thing the Princess' overtired, oversensitive ego could accept.

This was not a good way to spend the first months of her baby's life, and it all played on the Princess' own unsupportive beliefs about being incapable of dealing with her own life and not being good enough as a new parent. She thought accepting support would only prove this fact. The other problem was that the Queen was trying to help the Princess avoid the parenting mistakes she felt she had made with the Princess and her younger sister; plus, the Queen wanted to help in her way, without asking the Princess what she truly needed.

Neither of them effectively communicated what they really wanted, needed, or were trying to do, and in the end they were both hurt and resentful of the other: the Queen by the Princess' unwillingness to accept support, and the Princess by her own perceptions of the Queen imposing her way. Only through talking about what each was feeling did the situation turn into support as they both learned to ask for what they really wanted and needed.

This is a classic example of right person, wrong support. In my case, my mom was the perfect person to support me during my early parenting days. She was so in love with her beautiful, red-headed, first granddaughter, that she wanted to do everything she possibly could to make our lives better. It's just that the support she was providing was what she thought I needed, not the support I actually did need. Because of my stubborn independence (which she taught me), I was not willing to ask for or allow support, which left her guessing at what I needed. She then went ahead and provided it before I could let her know my actual needs.

As mentioned, parents often do this for their children, trying to solve problems or protect them without asking if they want or need their problem solved or to be protected. When children are young, this is a sign of good parenting, but as kids grow up, they sometimes see this parental involvement as interference.

When we anticipate an individual's need incorrectly, or do something different than they expected because he or she may not have communicated clearly enough, it looks like we're trying to take over and be overbearing or controlling, which is usually not the case at all. The thought most often is one of simply wanting to help and make life easier for the other person. It's just not the kind of support the other person really wanted in the first place. Right person, wrong support. In the end, remember that **how we as individuals perceive the**

Embracing Support

offered support will affect how much of it we accept and whether we'll ask for support again. The choice is yours.

"Whatever life is throwing your way, recognize that you, and you alone, choose how you are going to feel about it."
∞ *Unknown* ∞

The Right Way

How you ask for support is just as important as whom you ask. To be sure you're asking "the right way," it's helpful to understand how the other person communicates. Sometimes you may think you've asked clearly, but the message may be lost on the person you're asking. Sometimes, I actually ask the person to repeat my support request back to me. I'm not kidding.

I work with a person who is outgoing, talkative, and always on the go. Because of her communication style, I sometimes fear my requests aren't being heard. Her mind works in such a way that I will start a sentence and she will finish it before I get a chance to explain what I want her to do. Off she goes and does it her way. Sometimes this works well; other times it doesn't. We've had more than one setback when she doesn't complete or incorrectly completes a job. Sometimes, we've had to go back and redo the whole thing because she hadn't listened to the instructions. In these situations, I get to be self-righteous and tell myself, "See, I'm the only one who can do it." (Which doesn't solve the problem at all.)

Over time, however, I've learned to slow her down when we meet, and in those instances where it really matters, ask her to tell me exactly what she's going to do in her own words. This way I know whether or not I've clearly communicated my needs and whether she has actually heard what I've said. Sometimes we sit down and make a written step-by-step plan, so she doesn't have to come back and ask me again how to do it. We've solved a lot of frustration and communication problems this way.

I have also set clear boundaries around how much I am willing to support her. It helps when we create lists to guide difficult tasks. When she is having problems, I refer her to those lists instead of rescuing her or doing it myself. I have also stopped randomly voicing my complaints in the hope that she will help me with a particular concern. Knowing how she communicates, I learned she will never pick up on random comments. That will only get the attention of more supportive types of personalities (like me), who will take those complaints and try to solve them, whether we are asked to or not.

Understanding communication and personality styles goes a long way towards being able to communicate our needs effectively, and the research on this topic is extensive. Do you have people in your life that you have difficulty understanding or being understood by? I'm an introvert by nature, but I am very capable of taking on leadership roles when I pay attention to how others communicate. I've learned **when I'm not heard by others, it doesn't necessarily mean I'm not important to them** (like I believed for

Embracing Support

so many years). It has more to do with how we communicate with each other. Outgoing personalities often have difficulty slowing down and paying attention to quieter or more withdrawn personalities, because their brains are constantly working and planning. They often lack the patience to slow down and listen. In order to get their attention, sometimes we have to stop them and get them to focus on what is being said, which may mean asking them to repeat back what you've asked of them.

Likewise, very outgoing or more controlling personality types tend to want details and quick facts, so they can keep going with what they're currently thinking about or working on. When we try to communicate long, drawn-out stories, it's equally frustrating to them to have to listen to what they think is useless information. You may have some of these individuals in your life, or perhaps you are one of these individuals? The key in effective communication will always be to slow down, listen to each other and support each other in being understood. Especially when it comes to asking for support.

The Right Time

Timing is everything. When I am in an emotional crisis situation and need support, I may not be able to choose the right person or ask in the right way. I need support and I need it now.

When we have the time to plan for the support we need, it's easier to find the right person, but if we're in crisis mode (overwhelmed, frustrated, drowning, stressed by the intensity of the moment), we are more willing to take whatever support we can get at the time. This can sometimes be a difficult starting point for seeking support, but it is often where we find ourselves if we don't know how to ask for support or if we're unaware that it's okay to ask.

When we're drowning, we happily reach out and accept any lifeline that comes our way. Chances are at least some of it will be helpful. However, if we always use this approach to seeking support, we need to be accountable to this perspective and be willing to accept the help we've asked for, no matter what that support looks like or who it comes from.

Take a Break

Sometimes the stress and anxiety from our perceived current experience can lead to an emotional crisis. There is so much coming at us, or we feel like we have so much to do, that we end up in a state of complete overwhelm. However, often this crisis mode can be stalled if we can take even a minute to clarify exactly what we want or need. A short break might be all it takes to reframe our perspective on a crisis and start thinking about how to resolve it. Remember, **the experience of stress is the difference between our perception of what is and what we think should be**. Decreasing stress or averting an emotional crisis may be as simple as changing our perception of our current reality.

At work, I excuse myself for a bathroom break and take a few deep breaths before I go back to a stressful situation. Then I think about what is happening that is creating the stress or the emotional crisis, and reflect on what part of this situation I have control over. It's my own personal timeout. Even a short break allows me to go back with a clearer head and the ability to ask for what I need. This is a very effective strategy in nursing and teaching. It also works well when dealing with young kids.

At home, instead of yelling at the kids to be quiet when all they were doing was being rambunctious, I could go to the bathroom and lock myself in for a few minutes (provided they were safe), and calmly start thinking. Alternatively, I used to redirect them outside to play in the backyard for a while; I could phone my neighbor to see if they could go play there for a bit; I could ask my husband to distract them or quiet them down; or I could stop what I was doing and focus on them for a few minutes, because it's likely their interruptions of a time limited task were causing the emotional crisis in the first place. One way or the other, just a few minutes might be all it takes to interrupt the pattern of the crisis.

Meanwhile Back at the Kingdom

One day the Princess decided to take her two- and five-year-old trolls to visit the Queen in the country for the weekend. To prepare for the adventure, the Princess had to get a few things done at the castle, pack the weekend bags, and then drive an hour and a half to the Queen's lands (a.k.a. "the farm"). In theory it all seemed simple enough and the Princess thought she might even have enough time to catch up on a few things before she left the castle. In reality, however, she felt stressed and overwhelmed by the tasks before her. Before they could leave, the trolls had music lessons, the Princess needed a shower, and the trolls needed baths. The Princess felt like she had the most rambunctious monsters that day, because, as trolls so often do, they picked up on her level of stress and ran with it.

Everything seemed to take such a tremendous effort and an immeasurable amount of time. Even on the drive to the Queen's lands, the Princess felt like the trolls were unusually noisy and overexcited, and she was ready to strangle them. Realistically, however, the trolls were happy, excited, singing, playing with each other instead of fighting, and looking forward to the trip and seeing the Queen. They weren't overly noisy at all; it just seemed that way to the Princess because she wanted and envisioned some quiet time to reflect on her week, and was being overly sensitive to the trolls' behavior.

The Princess asked the trolls to be quiet and to settle down, but this was a clear example of asking the wrong person for the support she needed. The two trolls continued to chatter and sing in the back seat of the carriage. The situation built and built until they arrived at the Queen's land—where the right person to support the Princess welcomed them with open arms. The Queen was overjoyed at seeing the trolls and played with them and kept them busy while the Princess went for a long walk during which she could relax, clear her head, and unwind from an incredibly long and stressful week of ruling the kingdom.

If I had planned ahead, I could have decreased my

stress and avoided the crisis situation by asking my husband to help me prepare for the trip. With his support, I could have gotten some things ready the day before, I could have brought along some extra toys to keep the girls busy in the car, or I could have grabbed a set of ear plugs for me. If I had been able to decrease my own stress and anxiety at yet something else on a long to-do list, I could have enjoyed their happiness instead of resisting the fact that my needs weren't being met. In order to get the right support, I had to be clear on what I needed and ask the right person the right way, at the right time. Otherwise I would still be asking myself, "Why don't I have the support I need?" or more likely, "Why did I ever decide to have children?"

When to Ask for Support

What about you? Do you ask in advance, in anticipation of needed support? Or do you leave things to the last minute and then panic or feel rejected when no one is available to help? Are you aware that, when you wait until the last minute, you don't give others the opportunity to support you the best way they can? Leaving things to the last minute can sabotage the possibility of positive support outcomes.

For best results, plan for support ahead of time if you can, and set yourself up for success. In order to get the best, most useful support, try to anticipate what you need. Of course, this type of pre-planning can't always happen; sometimes crises just come up. But the more in tune you can be with the support you want and need, the less likely you'll end up in a crisis situation. It takes some practice, but it is doable, and there are strategies throughout this book that will help you get there.

A simple way to start is to **consciously take the time to plan your day, set boundaries about what you're willing to add to it, and stick to that plan**. We know we can accomplish a certain number of things without being overwhelmed. By planning out the day, we can ensure the support can be accessed ahead of time and will already be in place to make that day run smoothly.

Here's one more example to stress the importance of timing: I can't stand to be interrupted when I'm in the middle of something. Once I've finally focused enough to concentrate on a job, it takes me forever to refocus and get back to where I was if I'm interrupted. Interestingly, my kids, students, and co-workers seem to know exactly when the "best" time to interrupt is, and it absolutely drives me up the wall.

Over time, I've learned to plan my support to avoid these interruptions. If I needed a half hour at home to pay bills or some quiet time for tasks that require concentration when the kids were smaller, such as write a report or mark papers, then I planned to have the kids outside for that time, or to have someone else look after them to ensure I wouldn't be interrupted.

At work, I close my office door to indicate I don't want disruptions, and I negotiate a time frame with my students during which I will be unavailable. I proactively try to anticipate what they may need while I'm unavailable and take care of it before I shut myself away to work. By knowing the support I want and need during this quiet, focused work time, I can prevent the situation from becoming a crisis. I've discovered the better I get at setting these kinds of boundaries, the less likely I am to be interrupted, and the easier it is to get stuff done.

Of course, I still experience times when I feel stressed and frustrated, but it's usually because I didn't take the time to be proactive. I'm human after all. However, these times are less and less frequent, as I get better at asking for what I want and asking the right person at the right time. By having this communication in place, my husband and I support each other, and we are both happier in our marriage. At work I can communicate what I want and need from co-workers, students, or patients. By setting reasonable limits on my time, everyone's day goes smoother.

Activity: Stress Reduction

I encourage you to think about the types of emotional crises that may come up in your life. Are you usually plagued by work, home life, or family crises (stress, overwhelm, frustration, anger, resentment, too much to do in not enough time, etc.)? Take a few minutes now to really think about how support in these areas will create more happiness and empowerment.

∞ What are the most common causes of stress or overwhelm in your life?

_____
_____
_____
_____
_____

∞ What support would help reduce the possibility of these situations? Think about if there are things you could do to not only prevent the situation from becoming a crisis, but to potentially prevent it from happening in the first place.

_____
_____
_____
_____
_____
_____
_____

∞ Who can best provide this support for you?

_____
_____
_____
_____
_____
_____

∞ What support can they give you in these situations?

_____
_____
_____
_____
_____
_____

Embracing Support

- ∞ What can you do additionally, including potentially setting boundaries, to help prevent the stressful situation from arising?

_____
_____
_____
_____
_____
_____

- ∞ When the stressful situation does happen, what can you do, including potentially setting boundaries, to prevent it from turning into a crisis?

_____
_____
_____
_____
_____
_____

There are similar questions in upcoming chapters. However, reflecting on the role of support in avoiding a crisis now will help you apply some of the information presented earlier, and then we can keep adding to it. Plus, you will be able to start changing some of these stressful situations right away.

Control

There is one last thing I'd like you to consider

before we move on to learning about beliefs and how they affect support, and that's how your perception of your control of a situation can affect its outcome. In *Reframe Your Blame: How to be Personally Accountable*, Jay Fiset explains how control influences and affects our lives. He explains that **the only things we really have control over in our lives are our thoughts (beliefs), actions (behaviors), and feelings (emotions)**. Everything else in the world has an effect on us, but we have no control over it, only influence.

When you think about a crisis situation from this perspective, you can understand the aspects of it that you can control. When you feel frustrated or overwhelmed, how much of the situation is truly within your circle of control? You can only be accountable for and take control of your thoughts, feelings, and behaviors. With this in mind, you can then choose how you *react* to the situation.

I've asked you to start thinking about the type of support you could put in place to prevent that situation from becoming a crisis. If a lot of your crisis situations occur because you react to a situation rather than proactively prevent it, perhaps the biggest support you can give yourself is to stop the reaction cycle and learn to choose your behaviors instead. This is an interesting and very powerful concept that we will discuss further as part of the next Strategy. For now though, think about who can best support you when you do find yourself in a crisis of your own creation.

Remember that how and when you ask for support is just as important as who you ask. Consider that asking for support is not difficult; it just takes a little bit of thought and practice for you to get the best support possible. By being aware of what is going on in your life and then getting into the habit of asking, you will create a happier, more empowered, amazing life.

Finding Support

Here is one more activity to help you get clear on what you want, and how to get the right kind of support from the right person. Previously, we created a Contrast List of areas we were not happy with in our lives. I decided to add to this list. To help me achieve the goals in my "I Do Want" column, I created a Getting Support Plan. This is what the start of my plan looks like:

I Do Want...	Therefore, I Need...	I Can Find Support By...
– To receive genuine support because others believe in me	To feel supported by someone who believes in the same things as I do and can talk me through my self-doubt to create empowerment	– Asking friends and family who know what I am capable of to remind me of all I've accomplished at times when I doubt myself – Joining (or start) a group of like-minded people who support each other
– To easily set goals and create products to sell in my own business and to have	– To develop a strong business plan, with clear business goals – To make time to work at my	– Asking my friends who run their own businesses if they can recommend someone or an organization who can help me set up a business plan and start networking

a consistent income, with extra at the end of the month	own business	– Hiring a professional business coach to help me with a good start-up plan – Hiring a web designer to create my business website – Asking my friends for a brainstorming session on additional resources and support I may need or have access to
– To learn about abundance	– To spend time focusing on the abundance I have in my life	– Asking others to remind me about the abundance in my life – Consciously focusing on what abundance I have every day
– To believe and trust that others can and will support me	– To challenge my beliefs about who I can trust and ask for support by taking a risk (of rejection in my case) and asking	– Creating a list of friends whom I normally wouldn't ask for support, but definitely could ask – Talking to my coaches, family, and friends when I feel stuck or unworthy; ask for reassurance about my abilities

Activity: Getting Support Plan

Now it's time for you to create a Getting Support Plan. Copy items from the "I Do Want" column of your Contrast List into the "I Do Want" column below.

Embracing Support

Remember to be as clear and specific as you can. The more specific you are on this list, the easier it will be to find the right person to support you. If you can, name the people you have access to and describe exactly what they can help you with, or who they might refer you to. Don't limit yourself to just the people you know, and include other sources you want but haven't discovered yet. What do you need to get what you want? Take a few minutes now and complete the table.

I Do Want...	Therefore, I Need...	I Can Find Support By...

(Note: if you'd like a blank copy of this chart, go to my website www.healwithsupport.com/resources.)

Doesn't it feel great to get these ideas down on paper and feel clearer on the type of support you want and who you can start to ask to provide that support? I suspect now that you are clear(er) in these two areas, you feel a bit more open to asking for and receiving support. If that's the case, that's great, go ahead and ask. If you're still not able to take that step, that's okay, too. The next two Strategies are going to look at some of the beliefs that may be in your way and how you can work towards overcoming them.

So, What Have We Learned?
In this chapter:
- ✓ We've learned about reclaiming our power by making a decision.
- ✓ We spent time getting clear on how to ask the right person, at the right time, in the right way.
- ✓ We looked at who we usually ask for support and whether these people are truly the best people to ask.
- ✓ We learned when to ask for support and how the right kind of support can be difficult to find in a crisis situation, or when we don't give those who support us enough time to be able to support us.
- ✓ We've also briefly delved into accountability and how control and beliefs can affect support.
- ✓ We've added to our Contrast List to get clearer on how to get the right kind of support from the right person.
- ✓ We've looked at ways in which others can

support us and how we can ask for what we want and need to live a more fulfilling life.

We're getting clearer on how to get what we want and how support can help us get there. Now it's time to learn how to feel empowered and focused by taking a closer look at how the beliefs we have about our world and about ourselves affect how much support we have in our lives.

"Life isn't about finding yourself. Life is about creating yourself."
∞ ***George Bernard Shaw*** ∞

Strategy 3: Get Focused on What's Stopping You (Understanding Beliefs and Accountability)

"When we are no longer able to change a situation, we are challenged to change ourselves."

∞ *Viktor E. Frankl* ∞

We all have thoughts and beliefs about ourselves and the world we live in. Some of us are very aware of our beliefs; others are not. Our beliefs have a powerful influence on our lives and the situations we create for ourselves. (Yes, we create a lot of the things that affect and influence us in our lives—most of it unconsciously). As you read through the information in this chapter, pay attention to your inner voice—your self-talk—and to your emotional response to the text. These will provide clues to underlying thoughts or beliefs that you may wish to investigate further. The questions I ask here are designed to lead to new insights into your current life situation. My goal is to provide a solid foundation and support you to develop a greater awareness of your beliefs, so you can see how they affect your ability to ask for, accept, and allow more support in your life.

What are Beliefs?

In a compelling one-minute YouTube video called

Embracing Support

"Training Fleas," a scientist in a white lab coat places a large number of fleas in a glass jar and then seals the jar with a lid. The fleas jump and jump, trying to get out of the jar. Over time, the fleas seem to become aware that they cannot escape the jar, so they change their behavior, and jump only high enough to reach just under the lid. After three days, the scientist takes the lid off the jar but the fleas continue to jump only as high as they did with the lid on the jar. Not a single flea jumps higher. Not a single flea tries to get out.

Interestingly, when the fleas are released from the jar, they continue to jump in the same pattern, as if they are contained by the jar, actually maintaining their positions in the shape of the jar. (In the video, the narrator explains that even the fleas' offspring will maintain this behavior.) The behavior has become so ingrained that the fleas will actually starve because they do not try to break formation due to their "belief" that the lid is preventing them from doing so. The fleas are incapable of "thinking outside the jar."

While I recognize that the fleas in the jar experiment may or may not be true, and this particular video is part of an advertisement for PlayStation games from many years ago, many motivational speakers also use the metaphor of "training fleas" to encourage their listeners to think beyond current realities and test the limits of their experience. If we start testing limits, we can get a glimpse of what life outside the jar can look like. Sure, it can be scary, but challenging ourselves to see beyond the confines of the jar can also be very empowering.

Our Beliefs Act like Jars

My interpretation of this fascinating story is that we are often limited by our own beliefs (the jar), and mistakenly think our current reality is the only one available to us. Like the fleas, many of us get into the routine of, "that's just the way it is," and we stay in the jar, even when we are completely unhappy and starving (for food, love, attention, etc.) in our given circumstances. Our beliefs can be so powerful that some of us won't even try to reach for the lid, never mind the possibility of what's beyond the jar. If I hadn't started thinking outside my perceived reality, I would have never taken the risk to start writing a book. I would have listened to my old beliefs, which told me, "I'm no good at writing," and stayed in the jar, right where I was—miserable, unsupported, and creatively stifled.

The real kicker is that we often don't even realize we're in the proverbial jar, so how can we start thinking about reaching beyond the lid? Many of us are content (or not) with our current realities, saying things like, "That's just the way my life is," or "That's just how it's meant to be." Guided by this attitude, we can't even start to imagine life differently. Because we don't realize we have the power to change our circumstances, it is unlikely we will think about what outside the jar could look like. How sad to think, "I can't imagine anything different because I've never tested the borders of my current reality." That is how powerful and limiting our beliefs can be, and that is why it is so very important that we become aware of our beliefs and how they can limit our ability to live a happy and empowered life. The good news? There is a way out of the jar.

The Birth of Beliefs

When do we start to develop the beliefs that so heavily influence our behaviors? In the book *Actualizations: You Don't Have to Rehearse to be Yourself*, Stewart Emery suggests our beliefs about the world begin to develop the minute we are born (or even before) and that we base many, if not all, of our life decisions on these beliefs. He explains that we make judgments about our surroundings based on what we observe; these judgments become thoughts designed to protect us and explain why things are the way they are in our world. In other words, what we see and hear as children leads us to perceive the world in a certain way. Over time, we start to think of these perceptions as truths. These truths become our beliefs and provide us with a way to make sense of the world we live in.

In the book *Change or Die: The Three Keys to Change at Work and in Life*, Alan Deutschman defines beliefs as ideology, or the conceptual framework through which we view our world. Beliefs are sort of like the lenses in glasses that change how we see things. This ideology, says Deutschman, is a "complicated web of entrenched ideas that conditions how you think and feel." He further explains that our "belief systems" shape how we view the world, and that these "deep-rooted beliefs are [a] part of the 'cognitive unconscious'" that guides our day-to-day judgments, decisions, and behaviors.

As we grow older, we make new judgments about ourselves and our world, but often the original foundational beliefs we developed as children are still there and still affect every aspect of our lives and our conscious and unconscious decisions. These beliefs turn into patterns of behavior and these patterns can be very difficult to change, especially if we're not consciously aware of where the behavior came from or aren't willing to explore new patterns of behavior.

Many, if not all, of these beliefs are still very powerful in our adult lives and some support us in our daily lives. My own beliefs about good manners, dedication, persistence, and taking charge of my own destiny still serve me well, and have gotten me where I am today. But my fierce belief about needing to be independent has its drawbacks because it has limited my ability to ask for and accept support. In short, some of the beliefs we develop as youngsters continue to help us as adults, while others limit—or downright prevent—us from living happy, empowered lives.

Researchers have not reached a consensus about when we start to develop our beliefs, but based on Stewart Emery's suggestions above, and my own personal experience, I feel fairly confident in saying that many, maybe even all, of our beliefs about ourselves and our world develop during our formative years, as we try to make sense of the world around us.

∞ ∞ ∞

A friend of mine was abandoned by her parents when she was just five years old. When she shared this story with me, she told me that to make sense of her situation, she started thinking she must be bad and not worthy of love. This was the only way she could understand why the people who were supposed to love and protect her would leave.

This is how children cope with what they cannot explain. They create their own version of what must be true, regardless of reality. If these erroneous thoughts are not corrected, children will look for more circumstances that prove these thoughts to be true, and over time they become so ingrained that the children turn these false truths into beliefs about themselves, which can continue to influence them even as adults.

In my friend's situation, the thought that she was bad and unworthy of love lingered in her unconscious mind as an adult, and led to relationships that reinforced this belief and perpetuated her view of the world. Because she believed she was bad and unworthy of love, she attracted a man who treated her in a way that further reinforced how bad and unworthy of love she was through verbal and physical abuse. For years she lived this experience, until she finally became aware of her belief and where it stemmed from, through group therapy and personal development courses.

Once she became aware of the belief, her experience changed because she took steps toward consciously changing it. It has taken her a long time and much self-reflection and, at times, it continues to be a daily conscious effort, but she has managed to change her circumstances and her beliefs. Now she is an amazingly powerful woman who no longer seeks out people who reinforce her old foundational beliefs. Instead, she now attracts people who unconditionally love her for who she is, and she is able to unconditionally love herself.

"Those Who Love Me, Leave Me"
When I was a child of eight, I lost my dad through my parents' divorce. I missed him so much and saw

him so rarely that I tried to make sense of the situation by developing the recurrent thought that those I love will leave me. This thought was reinforced when my mom and new stepdad moved the family to Canada from Switzerland when I was eleven, and then again when my stepdad left my mom when I was fifteen. I lost a lot of friends and family through these many moves, and by then, this thought had turned into a belief.

    In my early twenties, the effects of this belief played havoc with my life. I went through one relationship after another, looking for Mr. Right. A clear behavior pattern emerged: I would meet someone, let chemicals and hormones take over as I thought I was head over heels in love with "the one," and then would watch as the relationship fizzled because, lo and behold, he wasn't "the one" after all. I became fearful of starting a relationship or becoming deeply involved because I knew he would eventually leave. On the other hand, if I did meet someone, and he was actually someone with whom I could have created happiness, and the relationship looked like it could turn into something long-term, I would find some excuse to break it off, move away, meet someone new, be too busy at work, or get sick and want to be alone. If they didn't leave, I would. Then I'd move on to the next relationship and would repeat the behavior pattern again.

    Over time I also realized the reason I was very lonely and desperately wanted to be in a relationship was because it meant someone wanted and loved me—something I couldn't give to myself. So, I kept trying, even when I knew full well the relationship was doomed from the beginning. I was almost thirty before I finally realized why I was recreating this pattern and repeatedly getting my heart broken. I finally learned to see beyond the behavior to the underlying belief: "Those who love me will, sooner or later, leave me." I realized I was the one who continued to recreate those circumstances, and attract those situations into my life, just to prove myself right.

How ridiculous is that? Why would I do such a self-defeating thing? Because I didn't know any better. I didn't know those beliefs were there, and that there was a different way to create relationships. I had no clue about how my unconscious beliefs were driving me to these behaviors. I could see other people in amazing and loving relationships that I so desperately wanted for myself, but I didn't know how to go about finding someone with whom I could start that kind of relationship. Someone who would love and accept me for who I was. Today, I still have a hard time trusting people and letting others get close to me. But because I am aware of this behavior and my underlying beliefs, I make a greater effort to challenge it, and I can tell by my behavior when the belief is triggered. Over time the effects of this belief have become much smaller and interfere less often.

"I Don't Deserve to be Loved"

At about the same time as I recognized my belief about loved ones leaving me, I discovered two other deeply rooted beliefs: "I'm not good enough" and "I don't deserve to be loved." These beliefs are the flip side of the coin in my serial monogamy relationships. You see, on the odd chance I did find someone who could have been Mr. Right, I did everything I could to push him away. Even though this caused me great pain over the years, my belief system wanted to be right, to protect me, and in its way, maintain my comfort zone and the safety of the "truth" about my world.

As backwards and paradoxical as it may seem, my belief system was trying to protect me from harm by creating thoughts like: "he's not the one," "he won't love me anyways," or "if he does, he'll just leave me." And the clincher, "I'm not good enough to be in a long-term relationship with him, because I don't deserve to be loved like that." So my behavior would change and sooner or later, one of us would leave, and I was proven right. Either he cheated on me, which proved I wasn't good enough to deserve his love, or he got fed up with my behavior and left, which proved to me that people I love will leave me, and, obviously, it's too hard to love me.

In one relationship, we were actually getting close to marriage, until my beliefs and fears got in the way. My behavior became extreme. Unlike my usual behavior, I overreacted to simple things—like my partner coming home late, or him not calling me to let me know where he was—in such an aggressive way that we constantly argued. If we weren't arguing, I found something to fight about or to blame him for. Fearing that he would leave me and hurt me in the process, I tried to push him away, so that I could protect myself emotionally. In the end, I recognized that this was unusual behavior for me, but I couldn't seem to stop and couldn't find a way to save the relationship. Recognizing the end nearing, I became depressed to the point that I was physically ill and immobile with grief for the loss and because I couldn't figure out how to fix the relationship or let it go. It took the intervention of my friends to get me out of that living arrangement, the relationship and the mental state I had put myself into. (Please note: This was my unique situation, and I am in no way saying physical illness or depression can be controlled by simply changing your circumstances or your state of mind. I only suggest for you to evaluate if such beliefs may be contributing factors).

The Wake-Up Call

It took this extreme experience for me to realize my approach wasn't working, I wasn't happy, and I didn't need to play that game anymore. I finally saw the behavior pattern and was willing to change it. Finally I took the time to be by myself and was finally willing to experience something different. After deep exploration of my behavior patterns and my beliefs, and the actions and reactions those beliefs led me to engage in, I finally realized what a messed-up world I had created for myself.

I knew I had to reinvent myself and create new, more-supportive beliefs and behaviors. I wrote new, more-supportive thoughts (affirmations) for myself to replace some of those unsupportive thought patterns and beliefs. I finally acknowledged that my thoughts of "not good enough" and "not deserving," and my fear of being left behind or abandoned were the cause of my unhappiness. Only then was I able to finally manifest a relationship that was different from all previous ones. The more time I spent examining and then challenging some of the beliefs I held about myself and about relationships with others, the better the relationship worked. That relationship lasted for two years and I began my journey to growth and change, including taking 200 hours of personal development courses to build greater self-awareness.

My Personal Development Fairy Godfather supported me in realizing how often I blamed others for my circumstances, and how little accountability I had for my own situations and relationships, so I started to change some of my beliefs. Unfortunately, my being accountable for my actions and choices created enough conflict in the relationship that it no longer worked for either of us; we had both grown and changed. As I became more aware of what I truly wanted in my life and in the man I was willing to commit to in a relationship, I realized that our goals and dreams were different and that we wanted different things in life. In the end, I realized that even though I cared for this man a lot, the love we had for each other wouldn't be enough to keep us together through marriage and raising kids. I wanted a partner to be at home with me, and to spend evenings and weekends together; him being gone for long periods of time because of work was not part of my vision of an ideal marriage.

That romantic partnership was an amazing growth experience for me and I am still very thankful to this wonderful man for the role he played in my own growth and change. The relationship was a huge step on the journey to my current happiness and empowerment. When we broke up, I initially reverted back to my old behaviors of blame and lack of accountability for almost six months and once again I became ill, until I caught myself and said, "Enough."

I finally drastically examined all of the beliefs I had learned I held (blaming others for my circumstances, feeling not good enough or not deserving, etc.) that were still limiting me from having everything I wanted and I continued to put new ones in place. I decided that I deserved an empowered life, and I chose to eat better foods and live a healthier life. I exercised regularly. I lost weight and gained strength. I listened to my heart and nurtured my soul. I found my creative side again and began to sing and write lyrics once more. I treated myself to a safety course and got my motorcycle licence. I went back to school and started my Master's program and made plans to move to New Zealand. I learned to appreciate who I was as a loving and lovable human being.

I was finally content to be me and stopped looking externally for the love and support that I hadn't been willing to give myself. I finally started to look after myself and to support myself toward a better life filled with love for myself and happiness with just being who I was. I decided I was the only one who needed my love and support right then and that I deserved every bit of it.

Once I finally identified the beliefs that were in my way, I was able to consciously work to change them. And because my relationship with myself changed, my context of what a relationship with someone else could look like changed too.

When I stopped looking to others for what I thought I needed and started giving it to myself, I attracted the one person who would truly be my partner. Two months after I stopped looking outside of myself, I met my future husband. I attracted that amazing relationship with the one person who could support me to give myself everything I ever dreamed about and wanted, and I was able to do the same for him. I had to find it for myself first though. Now, fifteen years later, I have this incredible, supportive, empowering relationship, a wonderful home, two amazing "princesses" of my own, and I feel more content and powerful than ever. It's amazing how changing our thoughts and beliefs about ourselves can change every aspect of our lives.

> *"It's the events in our lives that shape us. But it's our choices that define us."*
> ∞ *Mac Taylor* ∞
> **CSI: NY (Television Series)**

Foundational Beliefs: A Snapshot

My story illustrates some key ideas about beliefs:
- ∞ Our belief systems, or, as Jay Fiset calls it, "our BS" ("And it's no accident that it abbreviates this way."), develop to help us make sense of our world when we are young. The thoughts, ideas, and judgments we have about ourselves and our surroundings translate into beliefs that are designed to keep us safe in our world.
- ∞ Our belief systems (BS) are powerful enough to lead us to unconsciously create certain situations in our lives. Because we decide our thoughts are truths, we try to prove ourselves right, even if it causes us immense pain. The job of a belief system is to protect. It doesn't

recognize when beliefs are no longer beneficial—that we've grown and changed and learned new information about ourselves and our world.
∞ Underlying, unconscious beliefs can make it incredibly difficult—but not impossible—to change our behavior.
∞ To change a belief, we need to be both conscious of it and willing to examine the belief. In her book, *Belief Re-patterning: The Amazing Technique for "Flipping the Switch" to Positive Thoughts*, Suze Casey explains that we don't necessarily need to know where the belief originated, we just need to acknowledge that the thoughts and beliefs exist so they can be "flipped" to more positive ones.
∞ **Awareness through self-examination is the first step in changing a belief**. This can be done through paying attention to our behaviors and asking ourselves, "What might I believe about myself and my world that is causing me to behave this way?" Remember to ask for support with this step.
∞ Support plays an important role in helping us become aware of and change our beliefs. If we're clear on what we want and need for ourselves, we can then find the right person to help us create the change we want. Once we're ready to ask for support, we might find it's already there. We just need to choose to accept it.

Changing Our Ways

In *Change or Die*, Alan Deutschman explains that our circumstances are difficult to change because our beliefs have developed over our lifetime and are deeply entrenched. In the movie *What tнē #$*! Dө ωΣ (k)πow!?*, scientists discuss the neural pathways that bind our beliefs to certain behaviors, and how these behaviors cause the release of neurotransmitters (chemicals in our brains such as adrenaline, dopamine, and serotonin). In order for us to function in day-to-day life, certain neurotransmitters are needed (for example, serotonin elevates mood and affects learning and memory; dopamine helps with motor control, motivation, and arousal). They allow for normal and healthy bodily functions. However, when we have certain behaviors that we regularly engage in, or default to—such as being angry, upset, fearful, blaming others or consistently having high levels of stress—our bodies and brains become used to an excess of certain neurotransmitters that are triggered by these emotions. The more we experience these emotions, the more of these chemicals are released. Now think of it like coffee drinkers who, over time, need to increase how much coffee they drink in order to still be affected by the caffeine. It's normal for our bodies to build a tolerance to substances we are regularly exposed to, and when that substance is not there in high enough quantities—or not there at all because we're trying to not have that coffee, or we're changing beliefs and behaviors—we will feel like we're having withdrawal symptoms. Withdrawal can be quite unpleasant for some people, and thus we will unconsciously recreate more of those situations, where we feel these emotions, in order to cause our brains to release more of these neurotransmitters—similar to feeding an addiction.

In short, every time a specific belief is triggered, a chemical reaction happens in our brain and an automatic response occurs, which leads us to display specific behaviors, leading to further chemical releases to feed our addictions. If we want to actively change our behavior, we need to acknowledge the situation, and then consciously make new choices and become aware of the many automatic (unconscious) behaviors we engage in each day. By doing this consciously, we can build new neuropathways in our brains, and stabilize neurotransmitter release. As mentioned above, Belief Re-patterning can be a powerful tool to achieve this goal. I highly recommend Suze Casey's book or one of her interactive courses if you would like more information on effectively changing beliefs quickly and easily.

In *You Can Heal Your Life*, Louise Hay writes that the beliefs we have about ourselves and our world are simply a series of thoughts and ideas, and **any thought can be changed at any time.** *You Can Heal Your Life* contains an amazing list of new, more supportive thoughts (or affirmations) the reader can use to replace less supportive thoughts. I've also created a list of new thought patterns to help you ask for and accept support. You can access it on my website www.healwithsupport.com/resources. By repeating affirmations and through re-patterning of limiting beliefs, our old beliefs can be changed and new, more supportive, more positive thoughts will eventually turn into more supportive beliefs. It takes self-awareness, a willingness to change, and a strong support system.

Activity: Discovering Foundational Beliefs

Before you can create true change, you need to understand some of the beliefs you hold about yourself and your world. Use your current life experiences and your current levels of support to guide your responses to the following questions.

1. What do you think of when you hear the word support?

_____
_____
_____
_____
_____
_____
_____

2. What does your response to Question 1 suggest about your beliefs about support and having support in your life?

_____
_____
_____
_____
_____
_____
_____

3. Let's apply what you've learned about beliefs and behaviors to a specific area of your life.
    a) Choose one life area (physical, intellectual/ mental, emotional, spiritual, financial/ occupational, environmental, or social).

Embracing Support

b) List the **behaviors or habits** (both supportive and unsupportive) that characterize this area of your life right now or in the past. For example, for a long time, I have struggled with my physical weight and continuously find ways to be "too busy" to exercise. To answer this question, I would list all the excuses I have about my weight and lack of exercise and all the behaviors that keep me from achieving my ideal weight, but also include the things I do now or have done in the past to try to lose weight.

_____
_____
_____
_____
_____
_____
_____

c) Now write down the **thoughts or beliefs** that might be leading you to engage in some of these behaviors. Have you ever noticed that there is a pattern to your behavior? Do you remember what you were thinking when you started these behaviors? If you were very young, you may not remember, but that's a good indication a particular behavior may need to be changed.

_____
_____
_____
_____

d) Have you noticed any automatic (or unconscious) patterns of behavior that you repeatedly engage in that reinforce or are reinforced by your beliefs? In other words, is there a recurring thought each time you think about this activity or life area?

4. In life in general, what behaviors give you positive results? In other words, what behaviors did you learn (at any point in your life) that help you be successful (in love, life, career, family, etc.)? For example, I keep working on a project until it's finished, even if that means staying up late the night before it's due. This is an example of a more unsupportive behavior giving me positive results.

Embracing Support

5. How do you define personal success? Based on your behaviors, what beliefs might you have that have helped you be successful?

_____
_____
_____
_____
_____
_____

6. What beliefs or thoughts do you have that might keep you from being successful? In other words, what sorts of thoughts do you have that give you less than positive results in your life or keep you from being successful in these life areas?

_____
_____
_____
_____
_____
_____

7. How could support help you to have more successful thoughts and beliefs and therefore be more successful?

_____
_____
_____
_____
_____
_____

Insight into your unconscious thoughts and beliefs might trigger some strong emotions. Be gentle with yourself and keep learning. Once you've discovered some of the thoughts or beliefs that may be leading to some of your automatic behaviors, you can then start working on replacing them with new thoughts, and create new outcomes for yourself.

"It's the repetition of affirmations that leads to belief. And once that belief becomes a deep conviction, things begin to happen."
∞ **Muhammad Ali** ∞

Moving Forward with Change
The first step to changing unconscious automatic behaviors is to become aware of them. Then you need to stop the behavior, and finally, you need to consciously choose more supportive behaviors. During the personal development courses I took with Jay Fiset in 2000 and onward, I learned about becoming accountable for my actions and the choices I make in life, the "reaction cycle," and the "Stop, Look, Choose" approach. These three concepts play a big part in changing some of the limiting beliefs affecting our day-to-day lives. Under Jay's facilitation, I integrated the Stop, Look, Choose approach—which originally came from a transformational program called "The Gift" delivered by The Creators Code. Jay explained how our beliefs can put us into an automatic behavioral spin. We behave and react in certain ways, without ever considering the cause of our reactions. Unconscious and automatic reactions to situations are

based on instinct, created over time, and influenced by our beliefs. When we react to situations, we are anything but accountable for our actions. However, **if we stop to consider our actions, look closely at the beliefs that cause those actions, and choose a new behavior, we can effectively interrupt the unconscious pattern of the reaction cycle, and even become proactive.**

If I say, "I'm accountable for my actions," my intent is to become clear on the choices I made. Right or wrong, they are what they are. There is no blame or guilt; these are my choices, not someone else's fault. Accountability is a very important concept, and one that not many of us truly understand. It's easier to react to a situation—get angry or upset and blame someone (ourselves or others) for the current circumstances—than it is to acknowledge that we are in the current state of affairs because of the choices we've made in our lives, no blame attached. **Accountability requires us to look at a situation from a neutral perspective and ask, "What choices are open to me?" rather than blindly react to the situation and assign blame.**

Jay explained that blind, automatic reactions come from our BS and are linked to a lack of accountability. The reactions we experience are part of a belief that is triggered or poked, which is incongruent with what is currently going on, or with what we think should be going on.

Seven Steps to Accountability

To help you understand the relationship between accountability and automatic actions, let's take a step-at-a-time look at an automatic reaction I have.

I often become angry and frustrated when someone cuts me off in traffic. This is a blind, automatic reaction and often, I don't even realize I've become angry until after the fact. Let's take a careful look at this example—one step at a time. As we do so, you can apply the steps to an automatic behavior pattern you recognize in your life. Later, there is an opportunity for you to work through your own automatic behaviours.

Step 1: What is the event that causes the reaction?
I get cut off in traffic.

Step 2: What is the first thing that happens to you as you react to the situation? What other impact does your initial reaction have on your day-to day-experience?
Instant anger. I slam on the breaks to avoid a collision and then yell at the other driver and tell them exactly what I think of their driving skills and where I think they got their driver's licence from. (Isn't this a great behavior to model for my kids in the back seat?) Then I continue driving, but the next half hour of my day has been ruined because some idiot can't see over the steering wheel, doesn't check mirrors, forgot where his signal light is, or can't behave more courteously on the road when all I'm trying to do is get where I'm going in a safe and timely manner.

Step 3: When analyzing an unsupportive reaction to an event, think about the unconscious fears that might have come to the surface.
I'd ask: "What fear am I feeling right now that I'm expressing in the form of anger or frustration? What do I believe about myself and my world that has

Embracing Support

evoked anger in me?" I'm afraid someone else's carelessness is putting my passengers and myself in danger. On a subconscious level, I'm also remembering a near-fatal car accident I was in when I was 21. I was run off the road by a drunk driver who left the scene.

Step 4: Now think about the beliefs that may have been triggered during that event. Listen for the self-talk (in other words, what are you thinking or saying to yourself about this experience or the situation in general).

In my case, my beliefs include: "He wasn't looking out for me." "People who don't know how to drive shouldn't be allowed on the road." "I'm a good driver and I drive safely." "You didn't see me or pay attention to the fact that I was here, which tells me I'm not important to you." "I have a right to be here and to be safe," and so on. At the core is my belief: "I am someone who deserves to be respected," along with my unsupportive belief that, "I'm not important enough for others to pay attention to." (It's amazing, isn't it, how so many subconscious thoughts run through our minds in a matter of seconds, leading to unsupportive behavior patterns. Sadly, some of us wallow in these reactions for hours and days, and even take this behavior out on others.)

Step 5: Consciously choose whether this reactive behavior is supporting you in your day-to-day life.

In my case, it absolutely is not. Letting some inconsiderate gesture as simple as someone cutting me off in traffic ruin my day—or even a small part of it—is absolutely absurd and a waste of my time. (That's my judgment.) Yet, there are some people who thrive on such negative behaviors and need to have these experiences because they reaffirm the beliefs they have about themselves, and release more of those neurotransmitters in their brains. It's so very damaging to our physical and emotional health.

Step 6: Consciously choose to replace the automatic behavior with something more supportive. This takes time and practice, so please be patient with yourself.

For the most part, I've learned to catch myself at the point where I become angry. This is the "stop" stage of becoming more accountable for my actions. I become aware of my thoughts and behavior and immediately choose, on most days, to react differently. (I admit I often still think, "Idiot, aren't you paying attention?") Then I "look" at the situation and start to think about what might be going on for the person who made an erroneous judgment in driving etiquette. Maybe they're having a bad day and they're really late. Maybe they're preoccupied because they have kids in the car being noisy, they got some bad news, or maybe they're just inconsiderate jerks and don't care. This does not make their dangerous behavior okay, but I am empowering myself with these more supportive thoughts, and I choose to accept their behavior as *their* behavior, and am choosing my response to it. In the end, I'm accountable for my thoughts, feelings, and behaviors.

Step 7: Choose to forgive the behavior and then move on with your day.

Forgiveness needs to be two-sided. Forgive the

Embracing Support

other the trespass, and forgive yourself for your reaction, choosing instead to act differently next time. Over time you will learn a new, more supportive automatic reaction (create a new habit), and you'll be well on your way to changing at least one unsupportive belief and behavior pattern. Please remember, change takes time and practice. Be patient with yourself.

Remember also: the more willing you are to change, the easier your journey will be. Here's an opportunity to practice:

Activity: Seven Steps to Accountability

Step 1: What is the event that causes the reaction?
- ∞ Now think of a situation for yourself. What is a common everyday event that you have an automatic reaction to?

_____
_____
_____
_____
_____

Step 2: What is the first thing that happens to you as you react to the situation? What other impact does your initial reaction have on your day-to day-experience?

_____
_____
_____

Step 3: When analyzing an unsupportive reaction to an event, think about the unconscious fears that might have come to the surface.
- ∞ What fears might you have that may have triggered this automatic response? What other limiting thoughts are you thinking at this time?

Step 4: Now think about the beliefs that may have been triggered during that event. Listen for the self-talk.
- ∞ What are you thinking or saying to yourself about this experience or the situation in general?

Step 5: Consciously choose whether this reactive behavior is supporting you in your day-to-day life.
- ∞ Does your automatic reaction bring you positive results? If you could choose a different outcome to this situation, what would you like it to be?

_____
_____
_____
_____
_____
_____

Step 6: Consciously choose to replace the automatic behavior with something more supportive.
- ∞ How would you prefer to respond instead? What can you do to become more conscious of your automatic behavior, and then consciously choose a different one until you have built a new habit? Remember, this takes time and practice, so please be patient with yourself.

_____
_____
_____
_____
_____
_____

Step 7: Choose to forgive the behavior and then move on with your day.
  ∞ Repeat after me: "I forgive you for . . ." I forgive myself for . . ."

_____
_____
_____
_____
_____
_____

When we choose to become aware of automatic behaviors and acknowledge our feelings and thoughts—and consciously release them with forgiveness—our thoughts become lighter and we feel happier and more empowered.

> *"Above all, be the heroine of your life, not the victim."*
> ∞ ***Nora Ephron*** ∞

This step-by-step approach to reflecting on automatic behaviors is a good way to start thinking about your beliefs and becoming aware of a few key things that might be affecting the experiences you currently have in your life. It's a great exercise you can do any time you notice a behavior pattern for which you want to find the underlying thoughts and beliefs, and consciously start changing them.

To stop an automatic reaction, we need to be accountable for our *re*action and Stop, Look, Choose a different behavior instead. (The Seven Steps to

Embracing Support

Accountability process also applies to support, and we'll work through a similar process again in an upcoming section.) This activity is meant to bring awareness to what is happening within us at an unconscious level. Once we have greater awareness of our beliefs, we can be accountable in our lives and *choose* the experiences we want to create rather than unconsciously allowing things to happen *to* us. We can then also look at how those beliefs keep us from having the support we want, need, and deserve, so we can live an empowered life. It just takes a bit of practice.

One of the easiest ways to start is to ask, "What was that all about?" the next time you experience an automatic reaction. Then take a little time to consider the thoughts and beliefs that were triggered and led you to feel angry, fearful, frustrated, or upset. What was the underlying fear or frustration? There are powerful clues here.

Once we acknowledge them, each of us has the ability and the power to choose our thoughts (whether they are limiting or supportive), and with a bit of practice they won't be automatic reactions anymore. When someone says something hurtful, I can now think, "Ouch! That really hurt." But then instead of instantly getting mad and reacting, I can stop (by asking myself why the comment hurt); look (by asking myself if there is some truth to the comment, if it plays on a belief I have about myself, and whether or not it needs to be addressed or let go); and I can then choose my behavior (and either say something to this particular individual or ignore the hurtful words).

Pulling it all Together

Thoughts and beliefs that limit us are usually based on fears and can sometimes severely limit our success, achievements, and how much support we have. These beliefs are based on the unsupportive thoughts and ideas we have about ourselves and our world. Beliefs that support us (such as love, capability, and even stubbornness) have served us well in becoming the amazing people we currently are. Supportive (and sometimes even unsupportive) beliefs help create positive results or outcomes in our lives. The key to change is becoming aware of the beliefs you have from earlier parts of your life, so you can understand the feelings they evoke and the behaviors they lead to. Awareness is how you begin to change your automatic responses.

Making those changes may be a huge undertaking for some. There are many good books and courses available that will help you achieve a deeper understanding of your beliefs and how they affect every aspect of your life. I've listed a few on the Reference page at the end of the book, as well as on my website www.healwithsupport.com/resources. For the purpose of this book, however, we will focus on how your beliefs affect how much support you have in your life, and how you can use your beliefs, or change them, in order to get more support.

Accountability

In the previous activity, I introduced the idea of accountability and how we can consciously choose our thoughts, feelings, and behaviors. Now I want to take that discussion further.

I like to use Jay Fiset's definition of accountability: simply accepting circumstances as they are without attaching blame to the situation. The biggest gift I've ever given myself was to learn to choose how I react to a situation, and to choose my thoughts consciously, from a neutral and accountable (no-blame) perspective, instead of unconsciously reacting to a situation.

For example, one day my supervisor at work told me she would have to change my teaching schedule. She explained that a change in the schedule of a full-time instructor (who preferred to teach at the time I'd been assigned) meant some juggling had to happen. My supervisor told me I could keep my assigned number of hours, but I needed to shift them to later in the day. Knowing how courses fill up, I was pretty sure the later course would get cancelled and that I would most likely lose those hours altogether. As a full-time employee, however, the other instructor had seniority over my "casual employee" status, and therefore the change was going to happen no matter how I felt about it.

Initially I was very upset. I felt like I was getting screwed over and losing teaching hours. As well, as a full-time employee, the other instructor could teach at the end of the day when she was still on campus anyway, instead of me having to pay for additional child care. I was angry at how I was treated, and I felt disrespected, pushed around, and taken advantage of. I was very busy blaming my supervisor and the other instructor for taking away my hours.

However, that behavior was not accountable

behavior. After all, I had learned from my Personal Development Fairy Godfather that "all events are neutral" (it just is the way it is) and there is no blame. Instead, it's my reaction to the situation that makes it positive or negative in my opinion. **If I choose to be in control of my thoughts, feelings, and behaviors, I can consciously choose how to act and how to respond to a situation**, instead of unconsciously reacting to it. When I really looked at where my thoughts and behaviors were coming from, I realized they stemmed from my underlying beliefs and my fears. All things I have control over in order to become accountable.

So, what were my choices with my supervisor? I decided to look at a shortened work schedule as a gift. After all, I choose to work on a casual basis instead of full time because it gives me the freedom to work as many or as few hours as I want. I know full well there are no guarantees.

By spending fewer hours tied to my job, I would have more hours to write and create, learn something new, build my business, and spend time with my family. I also decided to remain grateful for the hours I currently do have, at a job I truly love. Working fewer hours in this job would also give me the opportunity to teach a different or new course, to expand my knowledge base, and learn something new.

By being accountable for my thoughts, feelings, and behaviors, I choose to control the only things I truly can control in my life (my thoughts, feelings, and behaviors), and I empower myself tremendously. By making a conscious choice about how I chose to behave, instead of unconsciously reacting, I tipped the balance of power in my favor, and I could work on creating a win-win situation.

What happened in the end? Because I maintained a good relationship with my supervisor by staying neutral and being flexible, I was assigned a better time slot, kept my hours and added a few, and got to teach a different course altogether—one I really love, that is a lot less work. Win-win.

So, What Have We Learned?
In this chapter:
- ✓ We've spent time defining beliefs and learning about how and why we still have some of the beliefs that may no longer support us.
- ✓ We've looked at how we can start challenging some of the beliefs that no longer support us.
- ✓ We've reflected on some of your own beliefs and how you may have developed them.
- ✓ We've learned about the powerful influence beliefs have over every aspect of our lives, including how much support we have.
- ✓ We looked at some possible reasons why individuals may not have the support they'd like to have, or what beliefs may keep them from asking for support.
- ✓ We've created some strategies for how we can change our beliefs to create more support in our lives.
- ✓ We've defined accountability and looked at how being accountable in our own lives can change our beliefs and lead to empowerment.

Before we put our new knowledge into practice, I would like to congratulate you on all the work you did as part of learning about this Strategy. I realize reflecting on our beliefs can be downright terrifying. (Trust me, I've been there.) I hope you continue to pursue this new awareness. There is power and freedom in becoming aware of what may be limiting you. You may find there are setbacks and that you revert to old behaviors. That's okay. It's just your old BS, trying to keep you safe in whatever way it thinks is best for you. I strongly encourage you to continue to become more aware. You deserve the results you create for yourself. Remember, you don't have to do this alone. You have support available to you, and support can help you HEAL.

"Forces beyond your control can take away everything you possess except one thing: your freedom to choose how you will respond to the situation."
∞ ***Viktor E. Frankl*** ∞

Strategy 4: Become Empowered (Understanding How Beliefs Affect Support)

"Stand often in the presence of dreamers; they tickle your common sense and make you believe the impossible"
∞ *Mary Anne Radmacher* ∞

Now that you have a basic understanding of how our beliefs affect most areas of our lives, let's look at how we can use our beliefs to become more empowered, starting with a closer look at the impact fear and trust can have. Fear and lack of trust can be hugely debilitating and limit us in our dreams and our successes. Experiences we've had and survived in the past will impact our willingness to try new things and take new risks just as much as limiting beliefs will keep fleas stuck in a jar. The interesting thing is that not only will fear keep us from trying, but fear and lack of trust will also keep us from asking for support. If we can get past our fears and learn to trust enough to ask for support, we will find ourselves truly empowered and supported. Let's have a look at how fear and trust can affect support.

Fear and Support

Fear has a great impact on our lives and is closely tied to our beliefs and to the way we ask for and accept support. In *Love is Letting Go of Fear*, Dr. Gerald

Jampolsky explains that each of us builds defences to protect ourselves from the hurts of the future, based on pains of the past. This is where beliefs come in. Our subconscious thoughts (beliefs) try to protect us from future, anticipated pain by reminding us of when we were hurt or unsuccessful in the past. Consider the limiting thoughts you might have. Do you ever think, "I can't . . ." "I'm no good at . . ." or "That's impossible . . ."? My own limiting thoughts include, "I can't draw," "I'm no good at art," "It's not possible for me to lose weight," and "I'll never be an emergency room nurse, because I don't think fast enough." Then there's the debilitating, "I'll never be able to complete a book that others might consider meaningful." Generally, these limiting thoughts are linked to comments we heard adults make about us or around us as children. They're words we heard once upon a time, assumptions we made about ourselves, or activities we tried in the past and weren't successful at. We make these judgments based on fear of failure (or success). Because we don't want to experience the potential pain of failure, we believe these limiting thoughts that run around our heads; we accept them as truth, even though they are someone else's beliefs.

    I strongly believe **fear is the only thing keeping us from living our hopes, dreams, and passions**. If I had no fear in my life and was sure of every outcome, I would have the confidence to attempt—and succeed—at all things. Fear affects self-concept and self-confidence and can even limit how big we dream.

    Fear of failure is closely linked to ideas about asking for and accepting support. If we fail, we might have to explain ourselves to friends, family members, a spouse or significant other, or our children. Our choice, then, might be to not share a dream or hope with loved ones in the first place, because we fear rejection. Of course, this means we won't ask for support either. If I question my ability to succeed, because I don't believe in myself enough, I don't want to share what I'm doing.

What many people in this circumstance don't see or understand is that asking for support is a way to work through the fear. The support from others will help you increase your own self-confidence and help you to keep moving to succeed in your dream. I can't tell you how often my fears kept me from moving forward. Yet when I decided to talk about it with the right person, they would encourage me and remind me that I am doing the right thing, and that I need to keep trying and doing. Consequently, I did. **Asking for the right kind of support to get past my fears made all difference between success and failure**. However, you do have to ask. And that may mean taking a risk.

"I'm Not Good Enough"

At about this point in writing this book, I started to stall. I had been writing and editing for about two hours one day, when I started to feel bored. I looked at the clock. "Oh, good, just past noon," I thought. "Time for lunch." Before long, I'd come up with all kinds of ways to take a longer break and all kinds of excuses to put my pen down for the day. I thought, "I've been writing for two hours already; I deserve a bit of a break. I'm going to read my romance novel for a while," knowing full well that once I started reading, I'd have trouble putting the book down. Then I started thinking, "If I'm bored writing this book, how could anyone be interested in reading it?" With that thought, I recognized my behavior pattern. I am so passionate about this topic, and see such value in it, and yet I'm bored writing about it? That is the dumbest thing I've ever heard of. I asked myself, "What is really going on here?" And I recognized the boredom as fear.

On other days, I found all kinds of excuses for not writing: I'm too busy at work; I need to chaperone the kids' field trips; I can't find the time to write; I have nothing important to teach anyone. Or I'd even experience physical pain that would prevent me from sitting and being creative. Again, I recognized these excuses were really telling me I was scared. Terrified, actually, of completing this project. Up to this point, my writing had been going really well. I had started to think, "Wow, I'm actually writing a book."

That's when another belief kicked in. This one constantly reminds me, "Who are you to think you can actually do this? What could you possibly have to offer someone else on how to have more support?" Initially I wasn't aware of this belief; all I saw was the behavior and the excuses I made for not getting this book written.

This is how fear shows up. Some kind of an underlying belief keeps us from doing what we want, which creates fear when we challenge it. Then our mind puts obstacles in our way so we stop challenging that belief and life can go back to normal. There are certain very specific behavior patterns that show up every time we challenge a specific belief. If I pay attention to the behavior patterns, I can start working on the underlying thoughts. For example, I know from past experience that pain in a specific location in my back is a physical manifestation of fear, because when I address the fear, the pain in my low back goes away instantly, without any treatment.

> *"Fear is the path to the dark side. Fear leads to anger, anger leads to hate, hate leads to suffering . . ."*
> ∞ ***Yoda*** ∞
> *Star Wars: Episode 1—The Phantom Menace (Film)*

Moving Forward with Support

In *Love is Letting Go of Fear*, Dr. Jampolsky maintains that two emotions underpin all other emotions: love and fear. He explains that the emotions we tend to think of as more negative, such as anger, boredom, guilt, and frustration, stem from an underlying fear; emotions we consider more positive, such as joy, elation, excitement, happiness, and so on, stem from love.

When I started to doubt my ability to finish this book, the procrastination, boredom, and stalling I experienced stemmed from fear. I used my inner support system to replace this fear with love and continued to work on writing with passion. I repeated affirmations and did some Belief Re-patterning to change these limiting beliefs into more positive and energizing thoughts. I listened to empowering and motivational music to help me stay focused, and I reminded myself how this information could benefit others. Most importantly, I reminded myself of the example I was setting for my children.

As I wrote, I thought more clearly about my own

beliefs and about the importance of support, which benefits my family just as much as it does me. I also called on a friend and I talked to my husband, voicing my fears, and asking for support to remind me why I was writing this book to begin with. By asking for support from the right people, I was able to be productive. I wrote for six more hours the day when I first felt myself stall. Then I rewarded myself by reading my romance novel until I went to bed.

I worked through this newfound belief using three support strategies: I called on my support system, I used Jay Fiset's Stop, Look, Choose approach, and I met with my Belief Re-patterning coach. This support network helped me identify and challenge the fear and the unsupportive underlying beliefs. With support, I had the strength to replace the thoughts of, "I'm not good enough" with more supportive thoughts such as, "**I am good enough. I am smart enough. I am valued. I have important information to share with others**." With practice, these new behaviors are now becoming so ingrained that I automatically work on changing the limiting thoughts, as soon as I identify what's keeping me from trying to be successful. In the end, having the right kind of support, and asking for that support, kept me writing this book until it was done.

Trust and Support

The power of fear to limit us is incredibly strong. Fear also plays an important role in our ability to trust others, which in turn affects how much support we have in our lives. I had an interesting experience a few years ago that illustrates the connectedness of support,

Embracing Support

trust, and fear and how this develops in children.

Meanwhile, Back at the Kingdom

Many years ago, the Princess decided to take her daughters on a long trip in a flying carriage to Switzerland, to visit her father, the King. On one fine, sunny Swiss day, the Princess took the little princesses to a nearby playpark. They soon discovered a new piece of equipment, consisting of a climbing tower, a slide, and a bright red fireman's pole. The princesses could climb onto the climbing tower platform using several different ladders and sets of steps. The fireman's pole was curved along the top where it attached to the wooden tower and then was a straight pole to the ground. All told, the pole was about six and a half feet from top to bottom—a tremendous height for three- and six-year old princesses.

The older little princess, Sonja, wanted to know how it worked. The Princess explained and then talked her through it and helped her reach across the span of a foot and a half to hold on to the bar, bring her legs over and around the pole, and slide down the way a firefighter might. It took her a little while to get used to it, but she wanted to try again and again until she was able to shimmy down that pole independently. The Princess finally had to stop her because the little princess was getting blisters on her hands from sliding down too fast, instead of using the appropriate foot positions and handholds to slow herself down. Overall, the little princess quickly realized her mom was there to support her and she trusted the Princess would catch her if anything went wrong. Throughout the learning experience, Sonja gained confidence because of her mother's support.

On the other hand, the three-year-old princess, Alexandria, needed help to reach across the foot-and-a-half expanse to the pole. Because it was just too far away from the platform for her little arms to reach, she would practically jump onto the pole and barely hold on long enough for the Princess to help her to the ground. The little princess had such unconditional trust that her mother would catch her that she just jumped blindly and was willing to attempt everything her older sister did.

At one point, however, the Princess was distracted for a fraction of a second, just to say hello to a passing couple (the polite thing to do on the playground), and didn't give little Alexandria her full attention. The little princess jumped as usual, and was nearly to the ground before her mother even realized she had jumped onto the pole to slide down. Fortunately, the Princess caught her precious little one just in time, and no one was hurt. But the little princess was much more reserved the next couple of times she went down, and much more insistent that the Princess stand there, watch her, and catch her. She actually stopped trying for a little while because it scared her so much. The Princess had to really encourage her to try again that day, so she wouldn't give up and be scared away from trying new things.

Whereas Sonja gained confidence with each "leap" and eventually went by herself, Alexandria seemed to become more fearful the day after the

Embracing Support

little mishap and much less adventurous. It took her a couple of days of going back to that park before she was willing to try again, but the little princess didn't give up and did eventually attempt the jump again. She needed the Princess' support and encouragement, and for a short while some hand-holding, in order to keep trying and attempt her leap of faith again. Once she regained confidence in her skill and ability, and in her trust of her support system, she kept going.

Now let's look at this experience from your perspective. Have you ever started a project feeling excited and energized, motivated, encouraged, and supported (even if only by your own internal support systems)? Then something happens. You get sidetracked by your beliefs about capability and accomplishment, or someone you thought would support you lets you down, or the support you'd hoped for never came to be, or you leap without looking and find that the person you thought would be there to catch you isn't paying attention and you fall.

At this point, most people choose one of two options. Some continue trying until they succeed. They reach inward to draw on personal strength or outward for new support. Eventually they achieve the goal they'd hoped for, with some struggles along the way. Others, however, use this experience to reinforce their beliefs, to prove they're not good enough, smart enough, rich enough, thin enough . . . whatever the limiting belief happens to be, and to feel so let down and disappointed that they give up on the project, and maybe even on their dreams. Additionally, because they didn't get the support they thought they would or because they generalize and feel they learned a long time ago that support wouldn't be there, they don't even reach for it anymore.

If you can see yourself in these situations, it's important to become aware of and stop your subconscious ranting or limiting self-talk. Instead, think about the type of support that might help, and then ask the right person for that support. You will be amazed at how fast you can work through your fears and change the outcome of the scenario. **Everything changes when you become conscious of your fears and ask for support**.

> *"Ultimately we know deeply that the other side of every fear is freedom."*
> ∞ **Marilyn Ferguson** ∞

A Matter of Choice

If you're aware of your thoughts and self-talk, you have the opportunity and capability to change your thoughts, feelings, beliefs, attitudes, and behaviors—if you choose. That is the key. If you're not willing to change your circumstances, nothing will ever change for you. If you want things to change in your life, and if you want more support and to feel more empowered, you absolutely need to become aware of and understand the beliefs affecting your life. Then be accountable in the choices you make. The good news is you have support available to you in the form of people who know and care for you (and sometimes from complete strangers who want to help others succeed, such as the coaches and other support listed on my website), who are willing to support you in becoming aware of these beliefs. **Your fear is the only thing standing in your way.**

Alexandria proved that to me. A couple years after her first misadventures with the "fire pole", I took her back to that playground. Then, at almost five years old, she re-discovered the pole and asked me to show her how it worked. Initially, she was a bit scared to try and I wondered if she had any memories of her previous experience. Once she figured it out, though, there was no stopping her. She did, however, insist I stay close to her, just in case.

How Beliefs Affect Support

As we've discussed, our beliefs are a powerful part of who we are. As I was struggling with my own beliefs about my ability to write and create a book that would be of value to others, I wondered where that particular belief came from. I thought back to an experience I had as a child.

"I Have Nothing of Value to Contribute"

I had an impactful first year of school. I felt that my Grade One teacher disliked me immensely, which may or may not have been true. I felt she talked down to me and treated me like I was incapable. Looking back, I realized this perception of my teacher and a series of unfortunate experiences that first year led to the unconscious belief that I had nothing meaningful or valuable to contribute.

You see, I used to press very hard with my pencil when I was first learning to write, which made it difficult to erase mistakes when I made them. I was told many years later that a psychologist once told my mom the reason I pressed so hard was because of my generous nature. (Personally, I think it had more to do with me wanting to make a mark in the world and to be heard.)

Because I hadn't quite gotten the hang of how to hold the paper in my notebook and because I pressed so hard, erasing mistakes usually meant I wrinkled, and sometimes even ripped, the page. Well, this just wouldn't do for a close-to-retirement teacher with a strict, old-school European standard. Thus, each time I made a mistake, my teacher made me come to her desk so she could erase my errors for me, without wrinkling or ripping the paper. My perception was that rather than supporting me by showing me a technique that would allow me to use the eraser properly and be independent, she embarrassed me every time I made a mistake. I tell you, I learned real fast not to make mistakes anymore. And ta-dah, a perfectionist was born.

To top it off, I quickly learned this perfectionist attitude worked in other areas of my life as well. I realized if I did things "right," I was valued for the work I did. It meant my mom (or whomever I was with) had less to do. My room was always neat and clean, I helped around the house, I was a "good" kid who rarely got into trouble, and I played by the rules. Now I was not only valued for my work, but also for my reliability and independence. As I grew up, people could trust I would take care of whatever needed to be done and they would never have to check to make sure it was done, and done right.

The detrimental effects of this learned behavior pattern, however, also meant I had to do it by myself (without support) so that I would be valued for my hard work and for being prepared. It took me decades to finally realize I could feel empowered by asking for help. One of the other problems that evolved was that this perfectionist became a relatively well-adjusted older sibling to a little sister who was six years younger and who never stood a chance at doing anything anywhere nearly as well as her older sister. A perfect example of how our behaviors affect those around us. Of course, my sister developed her own set of beliefs about what she was capable of, and what she is valued for. That's a book all in itself.

For me, though, the belief that I have nothing of value to contribute to others and that I have to do things for others to feel valued by them continues to this day. Fortunately, it no longer limits me anywhere near as much as it used to. Occasionally, at times when I am super busy with work and kids, I sometimes find myself so overwhelmed that I purposely don't finish things, because I don't believe I can achieve the high standard I expect from myself. Consequently, I return to my old behavior patterns and find myself with oodles of projects started, but too busy to finish any of them (because it would never be perfect anyway); my house becomes a cluttered mess; and I just have too much on the go to engage in meaningful relationships with my friends, family, or even my husband and children.

In these instances, when I find myself stuck in old patterns, support makes all the difference. I'm happy to say I'm a recovering perfectionist, and since I now recognize the behavior patterns and the underlying fears, my house is now mostly clutter-free (as much as can be with a 12- and 15-year-old), and I'm continuously and lovingly working on my relationships with myself, my friends, and my family.

"The most splendid achievement of all is the constant striving to surpass yourself and to be worthy of your own approval."
∞ *Denis Waitley* ∞

"I'm Not Wanted"

There is, however, another component to this equation. All human beings have an innate need to be loved and accepted by others. We seek their approval. Beyond anything else, that drives all behavior we exhibit and engage in.

One of the reasons I've struggled with writing, with friendships, and with support is linked to my innate need to be loved and accepted by others. As it turns out, I have another very powerful belief buried in my subconscious (surprise, surprise)—a belief that leads me to continuously question my value in a relationship: the belief that I'm not wanted.

I was never one of the popular kids in school. I was more the quiet rebel with hair in my face, ripped jeans, and rock band shirts and jackets, trying hard to fit in. Yet, I was never confident enough to actually live up to my look until I got older.

I still often feel like an outsider. I don't quite fit in; I'm not heard by others. Sometimes I still feel like others don't want me around, or that they just "put up" with me.

I continue to question the value of my contribution to a relationship and I am very hard on myself about how I interact with others. I second-guess my part in a conversation, and analyze it afterward, thinking things like, "Oh, I shouldn't have said . . ." or, "I should have behaved . . ." and so on. I also consciously choose to behave in ways that will lead others to comment on my value to them and how happy they are about my contribution to their lives. This is one of the reasons I began to teach and continue to do so. My students tell me how much they appreciate my teaching style and how wonderful the class is with me as the instructor. How much they've learned. In a sense, I give of myself, sometimes to my own detriment, to help others or to improve their lives, but it's all very self-serving.

In my early thirties I became aware of the belief that fosters this behavior. You see, I was a "surprise" to my mom and dad, and because of their family circumstances and societal pressures they promptly had a "surprise" wedding. I think I was about eight years old when I figured out I was born "two months too early." When my parents were divorced shortly after this revelation, I created my own version of their story and really started to question my value, and I asked myself, "If she didn't want me, why did she keep me?" I also used to believe that my parents would have never gotten married if I hadn't come along, and then they wouldn't have been so unhappy in their marriage and their lives.

Kids have an amazing ability to make adult issues their own. A friend of mine refers to this as "beliefs I accidentally took on as my own," which is exactly what I did. I decided to take on my parents' beliefs and make them my own, and that's how my life played out.

When I reflected on this belief, I could see that my lack of self-confidence and the way I interacted with others in the world were based on this one little belief—that I wasn't wanted. And if I wasn't wanted, how could I possibly have anything of value to contribute to anyone's life? That meant I had to work even harder to prove my value to them, which meant doing as much as I could on my own. If I considered this belief to be true, can you see how it would be difficult for me to ask for support? After all, how could anything I possibly want or need be important enough to warrant anyone else's time, energy, love, or money? My rationale was, if I'm not wanted then obviously I don't deserve to be loved and supported, do I?

This way of understanding my world was very real for me for many years. It is also one of the reasons I had so many dysfunctional relationships with people who would "leave me" or "couldn't love me." These were people who had their own issues, which I took on as my own.

The Upside

Along with the negative impact of my beliefs, however, they have also given me strength. I have done many things that others in my circumstances have not. Because of my beliefs, I became very stubborn and self-reliant; I have been on my own since I graduated high school; I put myself through school and completed my nursing diploma, my nursing degree, a diploma in gerontology, and a Master's degree in Education; I travelled by myself; and I faced and overcame several health crises.

This is an example of how beliefs that may seem

Embracing Support

unsupportive can actually support us and help us create other beliefs that serve us well, and help us be more resilient in times of adversity. Did I get to where I am the easy way? Definitely not. Had I held different, more supportive beliefs about myself and about asking for support, this journey would have looked a lot different, and probably would have been a lot easier. But I got here, and I'm proud to be here. These challenges made me into who I am today. I just wonder how much easier life could have been if I had asked for support, and had accepted it.

> **"What lies behind us and what lies before us are tiny matters compared to what lies within us."**
> ∞ ***Ralph Waldo Emerson*** ∞

Through the examples I've given, I hope you can see how beliefs affect the amount of support we ask for and accept. Or perhaps I should say "don't" ask for or accept. Understanding the thoughts and beliefs behind my behaviors has helped me understand why I tend not to ask for support, and that awareness has sincerely empowered me to have more support in all areas of my life. I've been able to make better choices since becoming aware of and changing my behaviors. I can now look at the beliefs keeping me from having the support I need and want. I can also set boundaries about what I'm willing to give to others. I can still be an incredible support to others, I can still fill my ego cup with feedback from others about it, and I can do it without draining myself.

Activity: Beliefs and Support

Up to this point, we've spent quite a bit of time looking at the link between foundational beliefs and support in my life, and you've had a chance to reflect on your own beliefs and how they impact your own experiences. Here is an activity to help you see how your beliefs affect the amount of support you ask for or accept. If you're interested in a blank version of this chart, or an example of how I would answer some of these questions, there is information available on my website.

Ask Yourself:	Physical	Intellect/ Mental	Emotional	Spiritual	Financial/ Occupation	Environ- mental	Social
Do I have all the support I could possibly want or need in each life area? (Y=Yes; N=No)							
In what life areas would having more support benefit me? (Check all that apply.)							
Would I see a significant change or improvement in this life area, if I had more support? (Y=Yes; N=No)							
In what areas do I want more support? (Check all that apply.)							

The Role of Support in Achieving My Goals

Embracing Support

1. Take a few minutes to complete the table above. Consider the role support plays in helping us achieve our goals.
    a) Using the completed table as a guide, ask yourself, "How could support change my experience in the areas I've indicated I'd like more support?"

_____
_____
_____
_____
_____
_____

At this point, you may wish to reflect on the questions you answered for the Personal View of Support and Getting Clear About Support activities as part of Strategies 1 and 2, and take a deeper look at the beliefs you have about asking for and accepting support. If you skimmed over the questions initially, you may want to delve a little deeper into them now.

   b) What's keeping you from reaching out and having all the support you want, need, and deserve?

_____
_____
_____
_____
_____
_____

2. Now choose one of the seven main life areas you identified in the table above: physical, intellectual/mental, emotional, spiritual, financial/occupational, environmental, or social. Ask yourself, "Is there anything I'd like to change in this area?"

   Life area: _____

   What I'd like to change:

   _____
   _____
   _____
   _____
   _____
   _____
   _____

3. What are some of your reasons (or excuses) for not being happy in this life area?

   _____
   _____
   _____
   _____
   _____
   _____
   _____

4. Take a moment to reflect on your response to Question 2. Can you identify one or more specific beliefs tied to any unsupportive thoughts, reasons, or excuses you've identified, which might be interfering with

your ability to have what you really want? What beliefs may be holding you back from making the changes you long for?

_____
_____
_____
_____
_____
_____
_____
_____
_____
_____
_____
_____

As you responded to the questions in the activity, beliefs may have become clear (or at least more obvious to you) if you reflected on what you wrote. Even if you just catch a glimpse of your beliefs now, that's still great progress. It just means we need to dig a little deeper. Keep identifying reasons or excuses why you're not happy in that specific life area, and try working on different life areas as well.

In upcoming Strategies we're going to look at similar questions in more detail and learn how to put more support in place. The most important thing at this time is for you to start thinking about your beliefs about life in general and support specifically, and to understand how they may be interfering with creating a happy, empowered, amazing life.

> *"Our past is a story existing only in our minds. Look, analyze, understand, and forgive. Then, as quickly as possible, chuck it."*
> ∞ *Marianne Williamson* ∞

A Different Perspective: Asking for Support

In the previous exercise you focused on your personal reasons for not asking for support. Have you discovered what some of those reasons are? I've also told you my story about feeling like I had to struggle to make an outcome meaningful and about being afraid to ask for support because of my fear of rejection.

Let's look at a very different version of why someone might not ask for support. A close friend of mine had an interesting view about support that was pretty much the opposite of mine. Whereas I tend to think I need to do everything on my own, and don't ask for help until I'm in dire straits and drowning, she used to ask for support quite regularly, for anything she felt she couldn't handle on her own. When we were discussing her thoughts about support, we uncovered a few interesting beliefs. My friend discovered she had a belief about being incapable of doing certain things. She asked for support quite regularly in those areas because she either wasn't willing to try, or she had tried and failed and was not willing to fail again. She said she would rather have someone else do it for her than feel like a failure. To a certain extent, I understood where she was coming from, but I also felt she was limiting herself in those areas. Those are my own beliefs about what she's capable of. I know her well enough to honestly say that if she really wanted to, she could be capable of many more things than she gave herself credit for.

Through our discussion, we discovered that by asking for support in all these little areas, she was testing whether or not those around her truly loved her. If someone was unable or unwilling to support her, she felt she was being told she was not worth supporting and thus not loved by that person, which was quite hurtful to her.

When she recently experienced a crisis in her life, she reached the point where she wasn't willing to ask for support again. She felt so completely overwhelmed that she was ready to "have a nervous breakdown." She had literally made herself physically ill as a way to test how far support (a.k.a. love from others) would go in her life. During our conversation, we discovered that her current crisis was simply another way for her to find out how much support and love she had in her life. You see, my friend also has an unconscious belief that she doesn't deserve to be loved. Her crisis was, in fact, a way of testing the boundaries of support and love in her life.

With each crisis, she was unconsciously waiting to see what it would take for people to turn her away and say, "Oh, that's just 'Lulu.' She always has a crisis, and I just can't help her again." My friend interpreted this message as: "This is where you draw the boundary after which you don't love me anymore. This is where you tell me that love is conditional and that I don't deserve to be loved." This is how she grew up, feeling love was conditional, and support was only available from those who loved her. The belief had evolved to the point where love and support were so intertwined, she could not separate the two anymore, and thus was continuously in a state of crisis, seeking support (and thus love) from others.

If you find yourself in a similar situation of asking for support all the time, I encourage you to consider the balance between relying on yourself and relying on others. Consider if you may have some underlying beliefs about not being able to do things on your own or having a fear of failing. Alternatively, you may be one of the fortunate few who already has that really awesome support system in place, and you have already discovered that great balance between asking and receiving. The rest of us are on our way to joining you. The key in any situation is to find the right balance between asking for and accepting support.

My beliefs about support and my friend's are at opposite ends of the belief spectrum. On one end is the belief "I don't deserve to be loved," which means I may not ask for support, out of fear of rejection. On the other end is the belief that "Love is conditional and has boundaries," which may mean I will continually ask for support, waiting for rejection. It's sad to see how misguided our thoughts about support can be and how much judgment we place on what we think others think of us.

Activity: Time to Reflect

By now we've established that when people don't get the support they need, it usually has something to do with their beliefs about themselves and about

Embracing Support

support, and with the types of people they ask for support. We've also discovered that not everyone will be able or willing to support us. We have to find the right person. It is important for all of us to have support, and it's wonderful that some of us already do. The key is to look at the circumstances under which we ask for support, and the meaning we attach to receiving or being denied the support we ask for.

This activity pulls together all the concepts we've covered so far to help you reflect on some of the factors or circumstances at play when you do or don't ask for support. For best results, give yourself time to reflect on the questions and answer as honestly as possible.

1. How often do you ask for support when you find yourself struggling in life, with a project, a goal, or something you want to do for yourself? (Circle the most appropriate response.)

Never   Rarely   Sometimes   Often   Always

a) If you answered "never" or "rarely," take a few minutes to consider what's keeping you from asking. Is it that you simply don't know how to ask, or is there something more that's interfering? Or maybe you're content with how things currently are in your life?

_____
_____
_____
_____

b) What might be causing you to feel like you can't ask for support more often?

_____
_____
_____
_____

c) If you answered "always," "often," or "sometimes," this is also a great opportunity to reflect on your thoughts and beliefs. Take a few minutes to consider what beliefs might be at play that lead you to ask for support as often or rarely as you do.

_____
_____
_____
_____

d) Under what circumstances do you ask for support?

_____
_____
_____
_____

2. What are the results when you ask for support? Do you usually receive the support you asked for? Give an example.

Embracing Support

a) Do you sometimes feel disappointed because you don't get the support you need? Explain your answer.

b) Do you ever feel there's no use in asking because no one is available to help? If so, consider if this is really the case.

3. Whom do you usually ask to support you?

a) Do you ever feel limited in whom you could access and ask for support? Is this really true?

_____
_____
_____
_____

b) Do you ever feel like you don't want to overtax your support system? If so, please also consider if that is truly their perception or your own.

_____
_____
_____
_____

c) What criteria do you use to determine whom to ask?

_____
_____
_____
_____

d) Do you ask certain people for certain types of support, or is there one main person you rely on?

Embracing Support

_____
_____
_____
_____
_____

e) Is this person always the best person to support you?

_____
_____
_____
_____

f) Who else could you ask for support?

_____
_____
_____
_____

4. How do you ask for the support you need? Consider: Do you make your needs known and then just hope to get the support you want, or do you clearly ask for what you want?

_____
_____
_____
_____

a) Before you ask, do you have a clear understanding of what you want and who can best support you? How do you decide who your best option for support will be?

_____
_____
_____
_____
_____

b) Where did you learn how to ask for support?

_____
_____
_____
_____
_____

c) Do you ask the right person for the support you need? If they're unable or unwilling to support you, what are your other options?

_____
_____
_____
_____
_____

5. When do you ask for support?

_____
_____
_____
_____
_____

Embracing Support

    a) Do you ask far enough in advance to allow others to support you? Or do you create situations that make it difficult for others to support you by asking at the last minute?

_____
_____
_____
_____

    b) How often do you find yourself in a crisis situation needing support? What are some potential causes of this and solutions to prevent it in the future?

_____
_____
_____
_____
_____

    c) When you're in a crisis and need support, on whom do you rely? Is this the best person to support you?

_____
_____
_____
_____

6. What beliefs are reinforced when you ask for support at the last minute and you do receive that support? What beliefs are reinforced if you don't receive it?

_____
_____
_____
_____
_____

7. What beliefs are reinforced when you receive the support you clearly ask for, or when you are denied the support you ask for?

_____
_____
_____
_____

If you've given yourself the gift of this reflection, congratulations are in order. Similar to working through the Seven Steps to Accountability, you can Stop, Look, and Choose, who, what, where, when, and how to ask for and accept support. You've taken a big step towards understanding your beliefs about support. The Time to Reflect activity you just completed is meant to help you get clear on what support means to you and the beliefs you have about different kinds of support, and to look at how often you ask for and accept support. If you need more time to answer the questions fully and honestly, take that time now. Alternatively, if you need some time to consider what you've learned up to this point, come back to these questions at any time. You may have gained a new perspective in the meantime. The main thing is, give yourself the gift of reflection on your beliefs.

If you're feeling a bit overwhelmed with this new

Embracing Support

information, recognize that what you're reading here may trigger a long list of thoughts and beliefs and some potential "should haves" and "could haves." If this is the case, please be gentle with yourself. You are learning powerful new information, which can have an amazing effect on your life. **Awareness takes time and practice.** It's taken me almost fifteen years to get to this point, and I constantly remind myself to be aware of my thoughts and behaviors and consciously practice applying these concepts.

We're nearing the end of the discussion on how beliefs affect your life, your happiness, and your empowerment. To really become aware of your beliefs about support, I encourage you to constantly ask yourself questions and look at your behavior patterns. We all see the world through our own lens or the filter of our beliefs. Sometimes it can be difficult to become aware of our own beliefs and see beyond the "flea jar" when these very beliefs could potentially be limiting us in the first place. Difficult, but not impossible. Spend time writing in your journal, reflect on your answers to the activities in this book and talk to a coach, or just a good, unbiased friend—anyone who will hold you accountable for your actions and choices. These strategies can make a world of difference in becoming aware of your beliefs.

Then, acknowledge that becoming aware of your beliefs can seem like a mammoth task—especially if you haven't spent much time thinking about them up to this point. **Many people never think about the reasons for their actions, thoughts, and feelings.** Many go through life content to experience each day like the one before, perhaps happy in the life they've created for themselves, or perhaps frustrated their lives don't change. Understanding the beliefs that shape your behaviors and thoughts will greatly help you to ask for and accept support. Growing self-awareness truly is the first step on your road to a happier, more empowered, amazing life.

"Remember, all the answers you need are inside of you; you only have to become quiet enough to hear them."
∞ *Debbie Ford* ∞

How Can I Change my Beliefs to Create More Support?

Now that you've spent some time thinking about the beliefs you adopted, many of them in childhood, you may be asking yourself, "How can I change my beliefs to create more support?" The process is straightforward, but may be a bit challenging.

I've given you a lot of story examples and questions to help you become aware of your beliefs. This awareness is the first step toward changing beliefs. Only when you know what your beliefs are can you look at replacing the ones that are not supporting you anymore. Resources such as affirmations and replacement thought patterns, or re-patterning limiting beliefs can guide you along the way. Every time you catch yourself thinking a thought that no longer supports you, replace it with a new, more supportive one. This will take some time and practice and some personal reflection. There are also a number of amazing personal development courses and coaching options available to help you uncover, understand, and replace your beliefs more fully and I have listed a few on my website: www.healwithsupport.com/resources.

The key to awareness is to be willing to change and reflect on your circumstances. There are lessons to be learned each day in our lives, and if we are willing to learn from them and take time to evaluate our thoughts and feelings through an accountable perspective, rather than from the perspective of blaming, our self-awareness will grow. With greater awareness of your beliefs, you can start to replace old thoughts and beliefs, and you are more likely to ask for and accept support from others. It will also become easier for you to be clear on the type of support you want and need so you can ask the right person at the right time. In turn, you will have more support in your life.

Activity: Visualization

Here's one more activity to help you become more aware of beliefs that may be limiting you from having all the support you want and need: visualize yourself asking for support.
1. Pick a life area you want more support with.
2. Close your eyes and imagine all the people you could ask for support with the situation.
3. From this mental list, think about the person you are least likely to ask for support. Ask yourself what it is about that person that makes you shy away from asking for support. (Don't just come up with a quick excuse, but honestly evaluate the scenario by asking: "What makes me not want to ask this person for support?

What beliefs are in my way of asking this person for support?")
4. Picture yourself asking this person for support for the situation you identified. What do you feel? What thoughts are running through your head? They likely range from absolute fear and terror to slight hesitancy; or perhaps you're not experiencing any emotions at all. The type of reaction you are having in response to this scenario gives you a clue as to how many and what sort of beliefs you may have about asking for support. The stronger the reaction, the more beliefs are potentially in your way.
5. Now, write down your answers to these questions:
    a) What thoughts do I have that keep me from asking for or having all the support I want and need?

    _____
    _____
    _____
    _____
    _____
    _____

    b) How have these thoughts and beliefs protected me in the past?

    _____
    _____
    _____
    _____
    _____
    _____

c) How can I change the wording of these thoughts and beliefs so they become more supportive and will help me ask for more support?

_____
_____
_____
_____
_____
_____

By reflecting on asking the one person who you would be least likely to ask for support, you gain further insight into some of the beliefs that are keeping you from asking for or accepting support in the first place. As part of upcoming strategies, we'll look at implementing all you have learned here and using the power of your beliefs to ask for and accept more support.

So, What Have We Learned?
In this chapter:
- ✓ We've spent some time looking at how our beliefs affect fear and trust, and how this can impact the support that we have.
- ✓ We've discovered that support can help us overcome the beliefs and fears we have about trust.
- ✓ We've added in more accountability and discussed our power to choose.
- ✓ We've addressed that not all limiting beliefs

have a negative impact on our lives.
- ✓ We've reflected on how we can change our beliefs to get more support, and how more support can help us change our beliefs.
- ✓ We've visualized how we can challenge our beliefs to help us HEAL.

You have done some powerful work in this section, and I commend you for sticking to it. Even a little awareness is a step in the right direction. Keep working on it and think about your automatic reactions. With time and practice, those automatic reactions can change, and new, more supportive behaviors can replace them. I hope you gained as much insight to your own situation by working through this Strategy as I have through the writing of it. By having greater awareness of your beliefs, you'll start feeling more empowered, and you're one step closer to creating a happy, empowered, and amazing life.

"Inaction breeds doubt and fear. Action breeds confidence and courage. If you want to conquer fear, do not sit home and think about it. Go out and get busy."
∞ ***Dale Carnegie*** ∞

Strategy 5: Change Old Behavior Patterns (Creating New Habits with Support)

"You will never change what you tolerate."
∞ *Joel Osteen* ∞

    Now that you've had an opportunity to take a close look at some of your beliefs, let's shift gears a bit and talk about behavior patterns. Behavior patterns can help you identify the underlying thoughts and beliefs that subconsciously lead you to behave in certain ways, thereby creating certain outcomes in your life. Your inner self-talk often provides clues to what these behavior patterns are. When you ask yourself questions such as, "Why do I always . . . (insert your repeated thoughts or behavior here)?" you might discover an unconscious belief at play that creates that specific outcome.

    In my past, for example, the question might have been, "Why do I always date men who don't treat me with respect?" The underlying belief was that I didn't respect myself enough and therefore attracted men who treated me the way I unconsciously treated myself. This is an unsupportive behavior pattern, and most of us have several. Fortunately I also have more supportive behavior patterns, such my habit to stubbornly finish whatever I start.

    No matter the pattern of behavior—supportive or unsupportive—it is based on an unconscious underlying belief. Statements like "I always . . ." or "I usually . . ." provide clues to understanding the behaviors that keep us from making long-lasting change in our lives. Once we recognize that behavior patterns exist, we need to dig a bit deeper to find out where they come from. I encourage you to discover the unconscious patterns of behavior shaping your life and then find a conscious way to respond to each situation and replace the pattern. When you do, you will discover great power and boundless support.

I've already shared with you some of my own behavior patterns regarding weight loss. Let's explore that a bit further. My pattern is I consistently stay up too late and don't get enough sleep at night. Not getting enough sleep affects my metabolism, which in turn affects my weight and the amount of energy I have for exercise. Other weight-related behavior patterns include consistently sabotaging weight loss by eating junk food late at night, avoiding exercise like the plague (often by being "too busy"), and out-and-out refusing to participate in anything that even remotely resembles exercise. My underlying belief about not going to bed stems from my childhood and has to do with not wanting to miss out on anything, but it also has to do with my belief about not having enough time to get everything done that I want to in a day, which leaves me feeling anxious and incomplete. In the evening.

Some of the beliefs I've mentioned earlier also keep me from losing weight: "those I love will leave me," and "the world is not safe." I believe extra weight allows me to protect myself by making me less attractive and less lovable. How torturous is that? I would have never realized I had these beliefs without looking at the behavior first. Now that I've discovered what my beliefs are, I can work at changing them by replacing them with more supportive ones: "I am safe in the world," "I am surrounded by people who love and value me," and "I am lovable and attractive." Being aware of my limits allows me to choose new frames of thinking.

Activity: Identifying Behavior Patterns

Now it's your turn. The following questions will help you learn more about the behavior patterns you engage in, especially those that may not be in your best interest.

1. Write down two or three of the behavior patterns (possibly things you identify as habits) you engage in that don't necessarily support you. (Come on. You know we all have them.)

_____
_____
_____
_____
_____
_____
_____

2. Each of these behavior patterns provide a clue to an underlying belief which may or may not support you. Choose one of the patterns you've identified above and try to determine the underlying thought(s) or belief(s) that may be causing you to repeatedly behave in this way. What might you think, feel, or believe about yourself that would lead you to this behavior?

_____
_____
_____
_____
_____
_____

3. And for the grand finale: What behavior patterns do you have when it comes to asking for or accepting support? Are these supportive or unsupportive?

_____
_____
_____
_____
_____

If you want some support with this activity, ask someone who knows you well to help you identify your behavior patterns. As an "outsider," he or she may have a clearer view of your patterns of behaviors than you do, simply because you may not want to acknowledge your own limitations. Before you ask, though, be sure you're ready to hear the answer—even if you don't like it. Remember: change can only happen through awareness.

Is It Working?

Reflecting on behavior patterns and the beliefs that lead to them is one way of clarifying your ideas about support. Another great way is to take a page from Dr. Phil's philosophy and simply ask yourself, "So, how's that working for you?"

When my youngest was five, she struggled for control and independence, which showed up as temper tantrums. Whenever she didn't want to do something I asked her to do (or if she wanted to do something I didn't want her to do), she scrunched up her face, stamped her feet, crossed her arms, and made a very loud, disgruntled "Humph!" sound. When she responded this way, I'd think to myself, "Here we go again." And I'd get set for battle. Obviously, I'd set off her delicate balance and pissed her off with something I said or did, or didn't say or do. The situation often escalated into full-blown screaming (on her part) and an angry reaction (on my part), especially if my attention had been focused on other things prior to our clash.

The usual consequence for a temper tantrum involved Alexandria choosing to give up one of her toys, sending her to her room until she'd calmed down and, eventually, getting her to apologize for her behavior. When she'd calmed down, we'd sit and discuss the other choices she could have made. Essentially, I was trying to reason with a five-year-old, which is about as effective as herding cats. Rather than resolve the issue, we were caught in a perpetuating, escalating cycle of behavior, with no end in sight. So . . . was that working for me? Obviously not—or I may have had some hair left.

I was at a loss trying to figure out how to deal with her behavior, and I knew at some level the pattern was contributing to her beliefs about herself, maybe about being bad, or maybe about not being in control, or not being loved, or not being good enough, or whatever else five-year-olds can conjure up (and believe me . . . the sky is the limit). And yet, I love her so much. All I wanted to do was teach her to manage her emotions so she could use them to her benefit, not her detriment. At five she was already such a strong leader; I wanted to make sure she was just as effective when she grew up. Essentially, I was trying to teach her how to Stop, Look, and Choose.

Interestingly, our pattern was also teaching her that temper tantrums led to one-on-one attention from me, which may have been all she wanted in the first place. Obviously, there isn't much incentive for her to stop if she gets what she wants in the end. With kids, behavioral outbursts are often just a way to seek attention that they may not be getting in other ways. In our situation, it was becoming a way for her to get my attention when she thought I was too busy for her, and this turned into a learned pattern. It was time for both of us to learn a new behavior pattern.

Breaking Down the Patterns

Who was my support in this situation? Definitely not my husband; he reacted even more strongly to my daughter's behavior than I did. I talked to friends and other moms about how to handle the situation. I read books, searched the Internet, and talked to my daughter's daycare staff. But nothing was working. I

Embracing Support

was starting to think that if I couldn't figure it out by myself, I would need to involve a professional who could teach me some new strategies for helping my daughter with her behavior and to help my husband and I to stop reacting to her behavior. After all, she was most likely just trying to express herself, make herself heard, and get attention.

Before taking that step, though, I decided to break down the behavior patterns to see if I could find out where my daughter was feeling unsupported and try to identify the beliefs that may have been causing her behavior. Finally, I had some success. In talking to her and observing her behavior, I came to some conclusions about her need for control. She was (and still is) a strong personality and hates being told what to do. She got bossed around a lot by her older sister, and often they argued and fought because of it. For my part, I started to ask her questions about whether something was done rather than telling her to do it, and I gave her more choices. For example, I might have asked her if she wanted to do her chores right away or in ten minutes. This gave her some control over the situation. I also looked at my own beliefs about how I used to feel when my mom would constantly tell me what to do, even though I had already planned to do it or started doing it. I hated that. Then I took a closer look at my beliefs about parenting and all the thoughts I had about what makes a "good" parent.

With time and patience, the incidents of our behavior decreased, and I'm happy to report that my hair grew back. My five-year-old learned how to use her words and to feel more in control. And I learned to stop reacting to her temper tantrums, to give her lots of positive feedback when she did well, and to give lots of hugs when she wasn't having a tantrum. Through a firm, loving, and consequential approach (with just enough humor to take the seriousness out of the situation), the incidents of temper tantrums decreased significantly and almost stopped.

How did this change happen? I talked to her about what I was doing and we planned ahead to avoid crises. For example, she started choosing her clothes at night (with feedback and discussion on the appropriateness of those clothes for daycare and school), not when we were rushed in the morning. We also started getting up a little earlier to give her more time with her morning routine of singing and admiring herself in the mirror, which made a world of difference, because she wasn't rushed and stressed any more. I became a bit more flexible, granting her requests more often, asserting a little less control over her and her sister, and intervening more often when her older sister was rushing her or bossing her around. Most importantly, I stopped giving her attention after an incident. We still talked about how she could choose different behavior, but the discussion focused on her behavior, not on me feeling guilty for instituting consequences for her behavior.

The best support I received during that process was from a close friend who encouraged me to think of my daughter as a loving, curious angel, and that I could observe her behavior from a neutral perspective, rather than allowing my emotions to direct my reaction.

Long story short, I started with a pattern that was obviously not working. I looked at the reactions we had to the situation and started working on identifying the underlying beliefs, both hers and mine. Then I was able to find the right kind of support for the situation and change it.

This is an effective approach for anyone wishing to change a behavior pattern. If you pay attention, you can become aware of how your behavior patterns provide clues about support that is missing in your life, and they will guide you to find the right kind of support. Once you're able to identify some of your behavior patterns, and observe what works and what doesn't work, you are ready to ask, "What would I like to change?" The Contrast List from Strategy 1 can be an effective tool to help you with this.

> *"It only takes a single thought to move the world."*
> ∞ **Unknown** ∞

What Would You Like to Change?

It is said that it is difficult for us to identify what we are lacking if we don't know we are lacking it. Similarly, you may have difficulty imagining what your life could look like with more support if you don't have support in the first place. Here's an exercise that will point you in the right direction.

Activity: Achieving Your Ideal
1. Think about the seven main areas of your life: physical, intellectual/mental, emotional, spiritual, financial/occupational, environmental,

and social. Imagine, if you can, what your ideal or perfect life would look like in one of these seven areas. (Note: Remember to think of someone whose situation you admire if you find it difficult to imagine your own life as perfect. What is it about their life that makes you think, "This would be the ideal life?") Now, describe your ideal life in the area that you chose. Be as detailed as possible.

_____
_____
_____
_____
_____
_____
_____
_____
_____
_____
_____
_____
_____
_____
_____

2. Considering your dream above, what type of support could help you turn this dream into a reality? Make a list of all the people and other resources you could access in order to live your ideal life in this area. For example, in my ideal world, support in the physical realm would

Embracing Support

include someone to help me make nutritious meals and someone to help me create fun ways to become more physically active and stay motivated to lose weight.

_____
_____
_____
_____
_____
_____
_____
_____
_____
_____
_____
_____
_____

3. Now use your current situation as a starting point toward obtaining what you consider an ideal life.

   a) Using the ideas you've just brainstormed as a guide, describe one thing you can do right now to start moving towards your ideal.

_____
_____
_____
_____
_____
_____

b) What does your support network need to be or do to support you in taking and completing this first step?

___
___
___
___
___

c) What qualities does the person who can best help you possess? (Answering this question will help you ask the right person.)

___
___
___
___
___

d) Do you know someone who fits this description? If not, where might you find such a person? Consider that you may not yet know all the people who could help you, but if you know what you want, you'll know where to start looking or asking.

___
___
___
___
___

4. Take the first step and ask.
5. Repeat.

This is an activity you can keep coming back to as your situation changes. Each time you do the activity, you can choose a different area of your life to focus on. Additionally, you can now go back to your Getting Support Plan and look at the list of all the people who could give you the support you want or need in those various areas and realistically evaluate this list. Your list may be longer than you think, and even if they can't do it themselves, they may know of someone who can. **You just need to trust them enough to ask.** There may also be a few things that you haven't considered up to this point, and others may have new ideas or strategies for you. Remember, anything is possible when we're not limiting our list by our own judgments.

Ask Anyway

As I was working on this section of the book, I started becoming more aware of my own behavior pattern: how I limit myself and often don't think big enough, or how I discount support from others because I decide they won't be able to support me. Regardless of whether that person is the right one to ask, I limit my own support by not asking. A good friend of mine commented that if I don't trust other people enough to ask, I don't give them the opportunity to support me.

My friend was speaking about a mutual acquaintance who could have been a great source of support to me in writing this book, but I hadn't asked her for support because I had already decided she wasn't going to be able to help me. I didn't trust her to be supportive in this situation. When I finally did ask for her support, it turns out I was right. She wasn't able to support me with what I needed. However, she did know someone else who was able to give me that support. If I had decided not to ask, I wouldn't have found the real support I was after. I had to be accountable for my own fears and mistrust, and set my judgments aside. Only then could I ask for what I needed, and then receive it.

Likewise, if at this point you're still feeling hesitant, remember that we've previously addressed many of the reasons, excuses or beliefs that can get in the way of asking for support. If asking still feels like a challenge to you, I strongly encourage you to go back to some of the previous activities and look at your behavior patterns to try to discover some of the underlying beliefs and fears that are keeping you from asking. The solution to not having enough support is actually quite simple: ask anyway. I promise you the world will not end if the answer is no (unless, of course, the question is, "Can you help me stop the apocalypse?"). Regardless of your thoughts about having to do it on your own, not having the perfect end result, needing to be in control, getting credit for your hard work, avoiding intimacy with friends and family, not trusting the other person enough to ask, having judged that they won't be able to do it based on your own limiting beliefs of what support could or should look like, not getting what you ask for, yadda, yadda, yadda . . . ask anyway.

Even if it feels like a big scary leap, imagine the

rewards of being in a supportive, give-and-take relationship. As I've mentioned before, most people are willing to support others and want to help in any way they can. So, ask anyway.

If you're having a difficult time imagining this, spend a bit more time observing other people who have support in their lives. It is so very important for all of us to have role models and to strive to expand our context of what is possible. What will help you the most is to **get clear on what you really want others to help you with, and then ask the right person for the task**. Take the risk and ask anyway.

Firing Your Support

It's also important to recognize when to fire your support. "Fire my support?" you ask. "But I've only just learned how to ask for what I need."

And that's a great place to be. However, being able to ask for what you want also means being clear and accountable on what you don't want. You need to be able to say "no" to anything and anyone who is unsupportive. You need to be able to set boundaries by clearly asking for exactly what you do want and clearly refusing what you don't want.

Usually, people respond to the idea of "firing support" in one of two ways. Some respond along the lines of: "I can't do that." "_____ (insert name here) will be upset with me." "I'll hurt their feelings." "That's my only support with . . ." But others think, "I didn't know I could do that." Or, "Can I really ask people to stop doing those unsupportive, energy-draining, unhelpful things?"

Yes! You can. The only thing standing in your way is your own beliefs about what support could and should look like, and your beliefs about asking for what you want and need. If you can get clear on your beliefs and on what you want, you can find support that truly is supportive.

Now, before you tell your mother her well-meaning gifts to the kids really aren't supporting you, please remember our earlier discussion about accountability and about having an open and honest conversation about how this individual can support you, or what changes may be beneficial to your individual situation. Please remember that when people get upset or defensive, it's based on underlying fears *they* have, and they may react angrily when those fears are triggered. Looking at others' behavior patterns can tell you just as much about their fears and beliefs as looking at your own.

I once had a friend with whom I was quite close. Over time, however, we saw less and less of each other. Eventually, we lost contact all together. The reason we grew apart was because I realized the relationship was not mutually supportive. When I spent time with her and her family, I felt neither supported nor energized. Rather, I would leave their company feeling drained and used. I came to realize that instead of supporting each other—the way good friends do—I usually ended up supporting her through her latest crisis, and she would want me to rescue her—emotionally, financially, helping her move, and so on. Over time, I came to realize this relationship was having a negative effect on me, and I knew I would never receive the support from her that I needed or wanted.

Embracing Support

After recognizing this, I decided to stop asking her for what she was unable to provide, and I "fired" her from my support system. Even though she really wanted to be my support, her situation was often one of crisis where she needed my support, not a position of being able to support me. I made the conscious decision not to ask her for support anymore, and to just to be her friend, without being her rescuer.

We remained friends for a while, but I limited the amount of time I spent with her, how much I was willing to listen to her concerns, and how much I was willing to support her. I tried to empower her to take control of her circumstances instead of just blaming others. We talked about the behavior patterns in her life and what beliefs may have led to the behaviors. For a while, she was willing to change some of her behaviors. Over time, however, we drifted apart and lost contact. The loss of this friend saddens me. However, I also appreciate the gifts she brought into my life through our relationship, and I'm grateful for having learned the importance of boundaries and conserving my positive energy, as well as finally asking for the support I truly needed.

"Most people are not going after what they want. Even some of the most serious goal seekers and goal setters—they're going after what they think they can get."
∞ ***Bob Proctor*** ∞

Meanwhile, Back at the Kingdom

After the Queen had her stroke, her income changed quite drastically, and she worried about not having enough money to run her kingdom. As a matter of fact, she had huge fears about not having enough money—even though these concerns were unfounded. Her fears stemmed from a belief she developed as a child growing up in a home without much money. So, even though her financial situation was stable (both before and after her stroke), she always chose to live very frugally, primarily because of her childhood fears and beliefs.

Being a loving grandma, she always showed up with gifts for the little princesses. Often these presents were toys and clothes from the second-hand store she volunteered at. Now, the Princess had no objections to buying second-hand toys and clothes, thinking that most clothes and toys are highly overpriced to begin with. But some of the gifts the Queen brought the little princesses were, in their mother's opinion, downright junk and dirty beyond cleaning. The Princess will be the first to admit she's very picky (and a bit overprotective) with the little princesses, so she decided to do something about it.

Because the Princess was still learning how to have an accountable conversation with the Queen, the first attempts at changing the situation were not effective. After all, the Princess loved the Queen and did not want to hurt or upset her. So, initially, the Princess came up with the excuse that she just didn't have room for all this stuff in her little castle, and she wasn't going to take it home. That sort of worked for a few months. The Queen stopped offering the Princess things to take home, but she continued bringing this stuff to her own castle and the little princesses were wearing those clothes and playing with those toys there. Ultimately, the situation hadn't changed. The Princess realized she had to be clear about what she needed from the Queen. The Princess didn't want the little princesses exposed to this stuff from who knows where, which after cleaning and bleaching still looked grubby and smelled like someone else's house.

 The Princess got up her courage and used her best communication skills, which she had learned in nursing school. She sat down with the Queen and said, "Mom, I know you love me, and I know you love the kids very much. Instead of bringing these clothes and these toys home for the kids, can you show your love by simply playing with them or by involving them in some of the things you're best at, like baking or painting? They don't need more stuff, just your love and attention. I worry that the things from the store can't be cleaned enough to not do them any harm."

 The Queen was a bit surprised at the Princess' request and, recognizing that this must have been bugging the Princess for a while, asked her why she hadn't said anything sooner. But the Queen also fully agreed with the Princess' suggestion that she could show the kids she loved them in other ways; that material gifts didn't mean as much as quality time spent together. And the Princess was able to voice her fear about needing to protect the kids and be clear on the type of support she needed from the Queen.

If things hadn't worked out so well, she would have had to fire the Queen as a caretaker for the little princesses or limit how much and how often she let them see each other, which would have been sad to see indeed.

The Unsolicited Supporter

As I've learned to ask for and accept support, I've also learned that many people genuinely enjoy helping others. They do so freely and willingly, without wanting anything in return, other than to feel good about helping someone.

Occasionally, though, you will meet someone who will feel insulted if you don't accept their support or advice—even if it isn't the support you need. It's important for all of us to be aware that this is their issue (behavior pattern), not yours. In other words, a person may offer unsolicited support or advice, and then feel rejected when you don't accept it. For them, providing support gives them an ego boost and they need that rush to feel good. When their advice or support is rejected (or just not needed), it triggers a belief in them about their self-worth. This is something they need to deal with, not you. Instead, be clear on what you want and be okay with saying, "Thank you for your (advice or) support. At this time, however, I don't feel like it's what I truly need or want." If you choose to accept

Embracing Support

their support simply because it's offered, consider if it's perhaps a useful starting point and then work towards finding what you truly want and need. Be clear with yourself that if you do accept their support, even though it's not what you want, you are settling for less than you deserve.

Activity: Evaluating Support

I've asked you several times up to this point to think about and be clear on whether the support you currently have is truly the support you need and want. I've also asked you to think about specific areas in your life where you may need more support. I'd like you to spend just a few more minutes on that scenario. Now that we've discussed behavior patterns and firing your support, let's take one last opportunity to evaluate the support you currently have and work towards changing patterns that may be preventing you from having what you want and need.

1. Do you feel you could make changes regarding the amount of support you currently have? If so, in which life areas would you like more support?

_____
_____
_____
_____
_____
_____

2. List all of the individuals, organizations, networks, virtual communities, and resources that you currently do or could have access to for support. The support might take the form of time, money, child care, a job, courses, massages, or contacts who will help you take the next step toward your dream. Think big. Remember, others may have new perspectives and new ideas about where you could get the support you want and need. Asking opens doors to resources others may know. (Don't worry about the possible limitations of that support. Just list them all for now. We'll get to ideas about the right kind of support a little later.) Try to list at least 10 sources of support.

_____
_____
_____
_____
_____
_____
_____
_____
_____
_____

3. Based on your list above, write down the top five reasons (or excuses) that keep you from asking for or accepting support from these sources. (Remember to pay attention to your limiting thoughts.)

Embracing Support

4. What have you noticed about your behavior patterns in these situations? Would changing your behavior allow more support in your life?

5. Who could help you become more aware of your behavior patterns and change the ones that are not supporting you? Make a list and include the behavior pattern(s) you would ask for their help with. How would you ask them?

6. Consider if there is anyone you may need to fire. (If "yes," carefully consider if you truly do need to fire them, or if you could simply ask more clearly for what you need and renegotiate the level and type of support you're receiving.)

_____
_____
_____
_____
_____
_____

7. What can you do and what can you ask your support system to do to ensure you are getting the right kind of support and creating a more supportive situation?

_____
_____
_____
_____
_____
_____

Remember that if you're clear on what you want and how you're getting in your own way, you're that much closer to having the support you want and need.

A Few Thoughts on Stress Behavior Patterns

Another important behavior pattern we need to look at is how each of us experiences and manages stress in our day to day lives, and how support can help us decrease the amount of stress we experience. Stress is one of the biggest health challenges facing Western society these days, and many of us are not adequately equipped to cope with it. There are greater demands on our time as we feel the need to be continuously plugged in and instantly available to respond to emails, texts and social media posts. Work and family time suffers, and many of us have become reliant on our devices. Our stress increases as we try to multitask. This constant engagement adds to what we see as our to-do list, and increases our perceived level of stress. Additionally, time demands as caregivers of children or elderly parents adds to our already busy lives, as we try to balance all our daily expectations. At the end of the day, there is very little time, if any, left to take care of ourselves.

Therefore, now is a great time to remember that the experience of stress is based on our perceptions. **We feel stressed when our actual experiences of an event are different from what we think should be happening.** It sounds pretty simple in theory, but can be a challenging behavior pattern to change. Do you recall reading about all those neurotransmitters floating around in your brain? Stress causes the release of those as well, and we can actually become dependent on them to the point where we no longer feel well when we do manage to decrease our stress level. We all know the detrimental effects stress can have on our health, in severe cases leading to heart attacks and strokes, and some research suggests even to cancer. Yet since stress is based on perception, let's look at how we can change our perception of a situation and reduce the stress we experience by asking for and accepting support . . . and as much as everyone hates to hear it, putting away the devices so we can start living our lives again.

A Reflection: How We Experience Time

For me personally, my biggest source of stress is feeling like I don't have enough time to complete everything I want to or everything I feel I should be able to complete. Then I finally learned that time really is an illusion and our perception of time is what gives us more or less of it. I learned this through standing still.

About a year ago, my daughter and I were working on her Halloween costume. She wanted the dress part of it to be black. Since we could only find something close to what she wanted in green, we decided to use some fabric dye to change the color to black. I read the instructions, put my mop bucket in the kitchen sink, filled it with hot water, and then stood there and stirred the dress in the fabric dye for 30 minutes, all the while thinking about everything I should be doing instead. It was the longest 30 minutes of my life.

Then I stopped thinking about my to-do list and recognized I had a lot of time right then to think about my relationship with, and my perception of time. How was it possible that standing still for 30 minutes felt like it took forever, but when I feel I have too much to do, 30 minutes goes by way too fast? I discovered that a lot of it had to do with the amount of multitasking I try to do, which unfortunately often makes completing tasks take longer because my brain isn't focused on the one task I'm working at. Instead, I started going back to my organizational tool and my to-do list and started focusing on one thing at a time. I found that I got a lot more done that way, and in a lot less time. Now, when I do feel stressed over time limits, I remind myself of the standing still experience and in my mind it feels like I can slow down time, just by remaining calm through taking deep belly breaths and focusing on the one priority task at hand. Everything else floating around in my brain gets written down to be dealt with after this task is done.

If your perception of time is a source of stress for you, I challenge you to stand (or sit) still for 30 minutes, and just tune in to your breathing and the power that your mind has to create peace in your body during that time. See if you can change your perception of time as well.

> *"Time is just an illusion, there is only the now."*
>
> ∞ ***Shifu*** ∞
> *Kung Fu Panda 3 (Film)*

Stress Management Basics

For further stress management, let's look at seven simple steps to help you reduce the stress you perceive and experience.

Step 1: Recognize that your feelings of anger, frustration, upset and tension are a sign you are experiencing stress.

How do you usually recognize if you're feeling stressed? What messages is your body sending you (e.g. headaches, tightness across the shoulders, upset stomach, unusual physical pain, cravings for junk food, etc.)? Recognition is the first step to change.

Step 2: Stop, take a deep breath into your belly, and logically look at what might be the source of the stress.

What is happening that has created the tension, anger and frustration? Is there a time limit involved which is adding to your experience of stress? What is your perception of the situation causing the stress? What is the unmet need you may be experiencing?

Step 3: Dig a little deeper. What other beliefs, thoughts or feelings are contributing to the situation?

Are you feeling incapable, not good enough, scared, lonely, taken for granted, unloved or not cared for? What else are you perceiving or experiencing at the time when you feel stressed?

Step 4: Recognize where the control is in the situation, honestly acknowledge what you do have control over at the time, and release control where you can.

One of the biggest sources of stress is when we feel we are not in control of a situation. How much control do you have in the stressful situation? Is there anything you can do to shift the control? Are there any areas where you could release control to decrease the stress you experience?

Step 5: Remember that you do have control over your own thoughts, feelings and actions, including how you perceive and spend your time.
Take back your control in the situation by changing your perception. Keep taking deep belly breaths to help you calm enough so your mind can focus on your thoughts at the stressful time. Then pick the thought that is loudest in your mind at the time of the stressful event. For example, my common stress thoughts are related to time and expectations from others, as well as my own beliefs about what I'm capable of:

"I have too much to do and not enough time to get it all done."

"I don't know enough to be able to get this project completed in the time I have."

"Why do I have to get all of this done by myself?"

"Why isn't anyone willing/able to help me?"

"I just need a few minutes without interruptions to get some of these many projects organized and something completed."

"I can't complete quality work when I'm rushed."

I suspect you have some similar thoughts when stressed, and now is a great time to recognize that all of these thoughts give the control to someone else. So let's take some control back and change some of these thoughts.

Let's change "I have too much to do and not enough time to get it all done" to "How I experience time and the amount of work to be done is my perception, which I can change at any time. I know I can ask for help and I can delegate or renegotiate deadlines."

Let's change "I don't know enough to be able to get this project completed in the time I have," to "It's alright for me to ask questions as I'm learning how to complete my new job."

Let's change "Why do I have to get all of this done by myself?" or "Why isn't anyone willing/able to help me?" to "I can ask for support if I want to, and I can keep asking until I find the right person to support me."

Changing our thoughts about a situation is very simple. You just need to become aware of them first. Belief Re-patterning of the thoughts and beliefs that lead you to feel stressed is also a very effective approach. Check out my website www.healwithsupport.com/resources for an example of how to do this.

Two other simple and effective strategies to taking back our control in any given situation come from Louise Hay and Jack Canfield. In *You Can Heal Your Life*, Louise Hay discusses an amazingly simple way to help you feel in control by changing the wording on some everyday statements we use too often. She says to start by writing down all of our "should" thoughts. Some of my common "should" thoughts include:

"I should exercise more."
"I should eat healthier foods."
"I should get more sleep."
"I should clean up the clutter in my house."
"I should make more time to care for myself."

When we look at these statements, all of them are disempowering and create a sense of guilt and stress for not doing what we think we ought to be doing based on someone else's expectations. These can

Embracing Support

weigh us down and create more stress in our lives. Instead, Louise Hay tells us to take our power back by reframing the statements into power statements. Cross out "should," and write "if I wanted to I could":
"If I wanted to, I could exercise more."
"If I wanted to, I could eat healthier foods."
"If I wanted to, I could get more sleep. . . ."
Or perhaps, "If I wanted to, I could ask for more support, from the right person, at the right time."

Now take your control back and actively make the decision to do what you think you "should" or want to, or just release the "should" by saying "I chose not to . . . (exercise, clean, rest, etc.) right now." Going back to Strategy 2, do you remember reading about Jack Canfield telling us to feel empowered by making a decision? Put away the energy draining guilt from "should" statements, and take control by making a decision. Which leads us to our second technique to take back control.

In *How to Get from Where You Are to Where You Want to Be: The 25 Principles of Success*, Jack Canfield explains the $E + R = O$ formula, where E is the event, R is our reaction to the event, and O is the outcome of our reaction to the event. Let's assume for a moment that all events are neither good nor bad. In fact, they just are. If your reaction at this point is, "What? With all the horrible stuff going on in the world, how can we say events are neutral?" take a deep belly breath, and hear me out. Events happen all the time. However, whether an event is deemed good or bad depends on how we react to it, based on our thoughts and beliefs about right and wrong. In other words, the event has no power until we attach meaning and react to it. Think about it. If you've just lost your job and are then in a car accident on your way home and break your leg, you will probably feel very upset, angry and stressed. However, if you've just received a 10 million dollar settlement after breaking your leg in a car accident, your reaction to the event will be much different, because there was what you may perceive as a positive outcome to the event. Thus, the event of you breaking your leg in a car accident is neither good nor bad, until you decide how you feel about and react to the event.

This same formula can be applied to events that cause us stress, by looking at how we react to the stressful event. We can look at losing our jobs as finally having a day off. We can look at deadlines as challenges we want to overcome. We can look at interruptions as a great opportunity to find out how others might solve the problem, and we can look at feeling alone and struggling as a great opportunity to ask for and accept support. We may even learn something new in the process. Regardless, in the end each of us gets to consciously chose how you want to react to the event, what you want the outcome to be, and how much support you want to ask for.

Step 6: Recognize the perceived expectations from others that we may have taken on as our own, and talk about them with the other person.

It is extremely important to discuss our feelings with the people who we think have the control in the situation, and try to resolve them using effective communication and "I" language. For example, "I feel ... when you ... " as in "I feel unsure of myself, which creates a stressful situation, when you don't give me all of the information I need to do my job properly" or "I feel taken for granted and unappreciated when you just assume I'll take care of things and don't ask me if I'm busy." Or perhaps "I feel incapable of performing to my best ability when I have too much to do and not enough time to do it in" (e.g. "when you rush me"). By using accountable "I" statements, we take the blame out of the conversation, take back our control, and acknowledge that we own the feelings and perceptions we are experiencing. This also gives the other person an opportunity to respond to our statements in a non-defensive way, without feeling like we're blaming them for the situation. This is just another part of being accountable for our thoughts, feelings and actions.

Step 7: Ask for and accept support from the right person

What beliefs are at play and in your way? We've spent a lot of time looking at what might keep you from asking for support. This also applies to asking for support in stressful situations. We've only added another layer to consider. So, what beliefs contribute to you feeling stressed? What beliefs are still keeping you from asking for and accepting support?

"The results you achieve will be in direct proportion to the effort you apply."
∞ *Denis Waitley* ∞

Activity: Seven Steps to Stress Management
Now it's your turn. Pick a stressful situation (perhaps the most recent one) and work your way through the steps by answering a few questions.

∞ What was the situation? Who were the individuals involved in the situation that led to the experience of stress?

_____
_____
_____
_____
_____
_____

Step 1: Recognize that your feelings of anger, frustration, upset and tension are a sign that you are experiencing stress.

∞ How do you usually recognize you're feeling stressed? What messages is your body sending you (e.g. headaches, tightness across the shoulders, upset stomach, unusual physical pain, cravings for junk food, etc.)?

_____
_____
_____
_____
_____
_____

Embracing Support

Step 2: Stop, take a deep breath into your belly, and logically look at what might be the source of the stress.

- ∞ What is the event that has triggered the stress experience?

_____
_____
_____
_____
_____
_____

- ∞ What is your current or usual reaction to the event?

_____
_____
_____
_____
_____
_____

- ∞ What is the unmet need you may be experiencing?

_____
_____
_____
_____
_____

∞ What is happening that has created the tension, anger and frustration? Is there a conflict of beliefs or values, or a time limit involved which is adding to your experience of stress?

_____
_____
_____
_____
_____
_____

Step 3: Dig a little deeper. What other beliefs, thoughts or feelings are contributing to the situation?

∞ What else are you experiencing at the time when you feel stressed? What beliefs were triggered?

_____
_____
_____
_____
_____
_____

∞ What thoughts and feelings are the loudest when you feel stressed?

_____
_____
_____

Embracing Support

Step 4: Recognize where the control is in the situation, honestly acknowledge what you do have control over at the time, and release control where you can.

- ∞ How much control do you have in this stressful situation? What can you control in this situation right now?

- ∞ Are there any areas where you could release control to decrease the stress you experience?

∞ What would it take for you to let go some of the control that might be contributing to the stress?

___
___
___
___
___
___

Step 5: Remember that you do have control over your own thoughts, feelings and actions, including how you perceive and spend your time.

∞ What is your perception of time? Do you have enough? Too little?

___
___
___
___
___
___

∞ What is the most time consuming event(s) in your day?

___
___
___
___

Embracing Support

- ∞ Do you participate in any activities that take up your time in a non-productive way? If so, what are they? How much time do you usually spend on these per day?

  _____
  _____
  _____
  _____
  _____
  _____

- ∞ What is your perception of the stressful situation? Looking at the thoughts and emotions that were triggered, which ones can you control and potentially change?

  _____
  _____
  _____
  _____
  _____
  _____

- ∞ What can those thoughts be changed (reframed) to in order to take back some control in the stressful event?

  _____
  _____
  _____
  _____
  _____
  _____

∞ What thoughts, feelings and actions would you rather be experiencing in a stressful situation?

_____
_____
_____
_____
_____

Now let's look at a few of your "should" thoughts to help you gain a sense of control.

∞ List 3-5 of your most common "should" thoughts that add to you feeling stressed.

_____
_____
_____
_____
_____
_____

∞ Now change these to "could" statements (If I wanted to, I could . . .)

_____
_____
_____
_____
_____
_____

Embracing Support

- ∞ How do you usually react to stressful situations?

  _____
  _____
  _____
  _____
  _____

- ∞ What beliefs may have been triggered that created or added to the stress of the situation?

  _____
  _____
  _____
  _____
  _____

- ∞ If the event causing the stress is neutral, how would changing your reaction to the situation affect the outcome?

  _____
  _____
  _____
  _____
  _____

Step 6: Recognize the perceived expectations from others that we may have taken on as our own and talk about them with the other person.

- ∞ Using effective "I" language statements, what could you say to yourself or to another individual that would help to decrease the stress experience? (Write down as many as you can think of.)

_____
_____
_____
_____
_____
_____
_____
_____
_____

Step 7: Ask for and accept support from the right person

- ∞ What support could you ask for that would decrease the stressful situation?

_____
_____
_____
_____
_____

Embracing Support

∞ What other support could you ask for? Who else can you ask?

_____
_____
_____
_____
_____

∞ What, if anything, is keeping you from asking for that support?

_____
_____
_____
_____
_____

I hope that working through this activity has given you some insight into how our beliefs can impact even how we experience stress. With a little practice, reframing of the stress experience can become quite simple, and you'll start to experience more peace and better health overall. Remember to ask for support (the right kind, from the right person) if you're finding stress management challenging.

Act As If

Here's one more approach to behavior patterns I want you to consider: "act as if." Let me explain. Jack Canfield discusses the success principle of "act as if" in his book *How to Get From Where You Are to Where You Want to Be*. He explains that if we act, think, talk, dress, and feel like a person who has already achieved a specific goal, this new way of being "sends powerful commands to our subconscious mind to find creative ways to achieve your goal." In other words, by believing you already have all the support you want and need, by mentally eliminating your excuses for not asking, and by physically doing what a successful person would, your brain will think you are already successful at this skill (creating an "inner experience"). You will start to actually create this experience in your life (having an outer "manifestation of that experience") without even consciously thinking about it.

Here's a powerful example of how this change in behavior patterns can work. In his book, *Change or Die*, Alan Deutschman tells the story of Dr. Mimi Silbert, a criminal psychologist who has quite a unique and successful approach to rehabilitation of ex-felons at the Delancey Street Foundation in San Francisco. This unique residential community houses ex-felons, prostitutes, hard-core drug addicts, and others who were given the option of incarceration or time served at Delancey Street. Residents are provided with educational opportunities—academic, vocational, and social skills—which are quite different from regular prison rehabilitation. Many of the individuals Dr.

Embracing Support

Silbert works with are second and even third-generation patrons of the judicial system, for one main reason: a life of crime, drug dealing/addiction, or prostitution is all they know. These were the behavior patterns they grew up with, it's all they believed they were capable of, and it's what was considered normal. Just like the fleas in the jar, these individuals had no concept that life could be different.

One of the steps Dr. Silbert expects her residents to partake in is to "act as if." Since the goal is to have the individuals in her care become well-adjusted, functional, and contributing members of society, Dr. Silbert expects the residents at Delancey Street to act as if they are well-adjusted, functional, and contributing members of society. She asks the more senior residents to model these behaviors for newer residents, expecting each one, from day one, to work and dress appropriately and use language a well-adjusted, functional, and contributing member of society would use. Through changing an individual's perspective on what is acceptable and expected, Dr. Silbert is able to expand the individual's behavior patterns and beliefs of what is possible, beyond what they know so far and have grown up with.

This amazing process can easily be applied to support as well. I asked you as part of Strategy 1 to think about others who have the support you want, and what your life might look like if you had that sort of support. As part of Strategy 2, we started looking at ways you can find the support that you want and need. Now imagine if you had that support in place. What would you do? How would you behave differently if you already had that support?

I know it might be hard to imagine something you've never had, which is why I'm asking you once more to think about someone who has what you want. Picture that situation and think about how you would act if you already had that support in place. Describe your new behavior here, and write down what your day would look like if you had all the support that you wanted and needed. What would you feel, think, dress, talk, and act like?

_____
_____
_____
_____
_____
_____
_____
_____
_____
_____
_____

If you have a clear picture, I challenge you to start acting as if you already have all the support you want and need. Amazing things can happen because our brains don't know the difference between our believing we have support in place and it actually happening. By changing your behavior patterns and functioning effectively, new beliefs can develop.

So, What Have We Learned?
In this chapter:
- ✓ We've explored what behavior patterns may be affecting the support you currently have.
- ✓ We've looked at becoming aware of our behavior patterns and how to change them to gain more support.
- ✓ We've reflected on your ideal life and how you can expand your current support system to include additional resources.
- ✓ We've reviewed whether or not your current support system fulfills your needs, or if you need to fire some of your support.
- ✓ We've explored how to manage unsolicited support.
- ✓ We've delved into our perceptions of time and stress, and looked at the impact of control on stress
- ✓ We've worked through awareness of stress and our stress management patterns
- ✓ We've learned about two very important strategics of "ask anyway", and the power of "act as if."

The foundation is in place. Give yourself a big pat on the back. Now it's time to start building to put a strong plan into action.

"It's your life . . . What you do with it makes a difference—and you control what happens to it."

∞ *Mimi Silbert* ∞

Strategy 6: Take Charge and Put your Plan into Action (A Step-by-Step Plan for Creating More Support)

"Keep in mind, just because you don't know the answer doesn't mean that one does not exist. You simply haven't discovered it yet."
∞ *Joel Osteen* ∞

Thomas Edison once said, "Opportunity is missed by most people because it is dressed in overalls and looks like work." I love this quote. It is so simple and to the point. Yet so many people don't understand its significance, and the same goes for support. When it comes to support, many people may recognize that they want and need (more) support, and they may even know whom to ask. But others miss the opportunity to ask for or accept support, simply because they don't recognize it as support. It doesn't look the way they think it should, it's not coming from the person they think it should be coming from, they're afraid to ask, or they simply don't know what support looks like or what it could look like.

I often find myself saying, "No thanks," simply out of habit, when someone offers to help me. The words are out of my mouth before I even get the chance to think, "Yeah, a little help here would be great."

In reality, **support is everywhere**. You simply have to be willing to consider the opportunities, become aware of your automatic reactions, and maybe

Embracing Support

step outside your comfort zone and allow support in. You can practice this with simple everyday things like letting the grocery clerks help you carry your groceries out, asking for help at work or at home, letting someone carry something for you when your hands are full, or saying thank you when someone holds open a door. The more aware of support you are, and the more you ask for and accept it, the easier it is to benefit from. It may mean doing something you've never done before—asking for help—but the end result will be getting something you've never had before—support.

You've done a lot of work up to this point, learning to recognize the kind of support you need and who can best provide it. Now we're going to put your new knowledge into practice and then celebrate your success.

Remember, changing our beliefs and thoughts about support can be challenging. Change takes time and practice. If you don't succeed in getting support the first time you ask, that doesn't mean you'll never get it. Keep practicing, and consider revisiting the activities in previous sections for a more in-depth look at the beliefs that may be in your way. Over time you'll get better at asking and finding the right people to support you at the right time. It will get easier. Be gentle and patient with yourself as you learn to pay attention to these new behavior patterns and ways of thinking, and apply them to your life.

What's Stopping You from Having Support?

I have addressed the possible reasons, excuses, and beliefs that may be preventing you from asking for and/or accepting support on several occasions up to this point. If you're still finding this to be a challenge, that's okay. It just means you need to spend a little more time and effort figuring out what makes this a difficult step for you.

I invite you to reflect on what you've discovered about yourself so far. If you truly do want more support in your life, it is absolutely essential that you understand at least some of the barriers that keep you from asking for or accepting that support.

Activity: Another Kick at the Beliefs Can

The following questions are a quick review and summary of some of the key questions you worked through in previous sections, and are designed to help you identify the thoughts and beliefs that may still be holding you back from accessing support at this point. You've discovered a lot about yourself since we asked those questions, and your answers may be different now. They may even surprise you. Remember to be honest with your answers, and really allow yourself to experience the thoughts and emotions that may be in your way

1. What has happened in the past when you've asked for support?

Embracing Support

_____
_____
_____
_____
_____

_____

2. How did you react when someone helped you? When someone didn't help you?

_____
_____
_____
_____
_____

3. How did you feel when someone supported you? When someone didn't support you?

_____
_____
_____
_____
_____
_____

4. Pick an instance from your past when you did not receive the support you wanted/needed. Consider: Did you ask the right person? At the right time? (Ask these questions about other instances as well.)

_____
_____
_____
_____
_____
_____
_____

5. What did you get to experience as a result of having support or not having support? What beliefs were reinforced when you didn't get what you wanted or needed?

_____
_____
_____
_____
_____
_____
_____

Your answer to Question 5 is particularly important. It will help you identify the beliefs that may be keeping you from getting the support you want and need. Take the time to answer clearly and thoughtfully.

More on Challenging Your Beliefs

You've identified some of the beliefs that are stopping you from asking for and accepting support, but how can you change them? One technique for challenging a belief is to do the exact opposite of what you would normally do in any given situation and then consciously replace the old belief with new, more supportive thoughts. This means really stepping out of your comfort zone and taking a risk. Through proving to yourself that you can do something, you empower yourself and further beliefs are challenged more easily. Here's what I did to challenge and change a belief in my life.

I used to have a belief that I wasn't heard and that I had nothing of value to contribute to conversations. What did I do to challenge that belief? I purposely did the opposite and started talking to people: I challenged myself to become a teacher—a university instructor, in fact. I sang karaoke, too, and I began to actively participate in conversations. The trick was to find the right conversations. I realized the reason I had nothing to contribute to a conversation in the first place was because I had no interest in what the individuals were talking about, or had little in common with them. Once I found the right conversation, this wasn't an issue anymore. Truthfully, I still feel awkward sometimes, but I'm okay with that, because I also know I love and value myself and I have value to others. Even though I'm a quiet introvert by nature, and prefer to listen more than I speak, I can now stand in front of a class of 100 students and keep them engaged, and I can carry on a conversation with strangers while standing in line at the grocery store. Belief challenged and changing.

"Success is not final, failure is not fatal: it is the courage to continue that counts."
∞ ***Winston Churchill*** ∞

Your Amazing Strategies in Action

This Strategy is all about building a step-by-step approach to creating support in your life. Here is where we start to put everything into action, and summarize everything you've learned so far into seven easy steps to provide a solid starting point for asking for and accepting support in your life.

Step 1: Know What You Want

Your Contrast List and Getting Support Plan have helped you clarify what you want your life to look like. The brief exercises here are also designed to help you discover why you haven't been able to achieve that life yet. If you've done the work in the last section and throughout the previous Strategies, you probably have a new understanding of what is in your way. If you're still not clear, you may need to go back to some of the previous activities or ask for support. Remember, if you want more support in your life, you need to be aware of exactly what you want.

In the space below, summarize the key points of what you want your life to look like, and the main beliefs, reasons, or excuses that tend to get in the way of you asking for support. Every time you write the details, the image of your ideal life gets that much clearer.

∞ I want:

_____
_____
_____
_____

Embracing Support

∞ I get in my own way by (beliefs, reasons, and excuses):

∞ Now choose one specific life area (from the "wants" you identified above) that you want to practice these seven steps with first. What specifically do you want in this life area?

*"Not everything that is faced can be changed.
But nothing can be changed until it is faced."*
∞ **James Baldwin** ∞

Step 2: Find the Right Person

Finding an ideal person to ask for support doesn't mean you can't ask anyone else, or that this is the only person who can support you. What it does mean, though, is the more qualities an individual possesses that align with what your ideal person would possess, the more likely you'll receive the support you need. Maybe you'll find those qualities in two or more people, or parts of them in various individuals, and you're that much closer to getting exactly what you want and need.

I'd like to add here that finding the right person is not as complex or difficult as it sounds. All you have to do is ask yourself, "Is this person capable of giving me what I'm asking for?" If you ask and don't get what you're after, chances are they were not, so stop asking and keep looking. Also, not finding the right person shouldn't stop you from asking others. Sometimes we judge people as not the right person and so decide not to ask anyone, thus keeping ourselves from potentially getting what we want. People will surprise you when you ask clearly for what you want.

Remember also, others have access to resources you don't know about. If you step outside your comfort zone and ask anyway, you may access information you didn't even know was an option. Additionally, being clear on who to ask will allow you to fire unsolicited support and stop wasting energy

Embracing Support

coming up with excuses for why you don't need their help. Instead, you can then direct your energy towards achieving your goal.

In the Getting Support Plan you completed earlier, you listed a few people or other resources who could support you. For the question below, remember to include the individuals and resources on that list here as well. Be clear and open. Here's your opportunity to pick, and work with, one specific area of your life that you want more support with.

In the space below, write the names of the people, resources, or organizations **that you think are most likely to provide the best support for the changes you identified in the previous question**. (Remember: You may need to ask more than one individual, access multiple resources, or do some further research to get what you want and need.)

_____
_____
_____
_____
_____
_____
_____

Step 3: Ask for Support (Act As If)

Actively asking for support can be simple, like making a basic request to family, friends, or acquaintances, or more elaborate, like placing an ad and hiring someone to do a job for you. Be clear about what you're asking for and make your request understood. Being clear on what you want to accomplish, what support you want and need, and what you want your outcome to look like, will play a significant role in how fast and easily you get results. Sometimes this means acting as if the support is already in place and asking anyway. Sometimes it means asking for the obvious.

In Steps 1 and 2 above, I asked you to think about one specific area of your life that you want more support in and to choose the person who could help you in that area. In the space below, describe the specific type of support you will ask for.

_____
_____
_____
_____
_____
_____

- ∞ Now challenge yourself and write down exactly how you will ask for support. What will you say?

_____
_____
_____
_____
_____
_____

- ∞ Here is another opportunity to describe exactly what your life would be like and how you would think, act, and feel, if that support were already in place.

Embracing Support

---

*"Believe and act as if
it were impossible to fail."*
∞ *Charles F. Kettering* ∞

Step 4: Ask for the Obvious

I can't tell you how often I hear people frustrated with their support system because they're not getting the support they need. Friends, family, co-workers, students, and patients and their family members alike ask me, "Why do I have to ask? Isn't it obvious that I need . . . ?" The unfortunate truth is that everyone thinks a little bit differently, that we're often busy and self-preoccupied, and it's usually only the more supporting type personalities that can anticipate what someone may need and provide it before the individual has to ask for it. So, the truth of the matter is: yes. As frustrating as it may seem, you do have to ask for the obvious, because most of us are not mind readers.

Meanwhile, Back at the Kingdom

One Sunday evening the Princess and her family came home late from a weekend away and there were many things that needed to be done before she could go to bed that night. Her husband, the Prince, helped her unload the car and get the little princesses settled in for the night. Then he went off to have a shower and get ready for bed. Meanwhile, the Princess was busy unpacking suitcases, getting laundry sorted, putting away the food they'd brought home, sorting through other items, and generally cleaning up before she could get ready for her next busy day. Only then could she think about getting ready for bed as well.

But her to-do list refused to become shorter, and the Princess became more and more frustrated and upset that she was doing all of this by herself. She thought to herself, "I shouldn't have to ask for help with this. Isn't it obvious that there is work to be done?" But you know what? It wasn't obvious to the Prince. He saw that the Princess was busy, but he had no idea what all needed to get done. Later, when they spoke of her anger and frustration at the situation, he said, "I had no idea that all that stuff still needed to be done. If I had known, I would have helped. Why didn't you ask for help?" She was still upset, so her response was, "I shouldn't have to ask."

The moral of the story: Just because it's obvious to you, doesn't mean it's obvious to the people around you. **We train people how to treat us and how to behave around us, and over time this behavior turns into habit**. My husband is more than willing to help out, because it means he gets more of my attention in the end. I just need to remember that we all look at the world differently, and what he sees is not the same as what I see when we look at the same problem. Remember, too, that a problem can be solved in many different ways. **So, save yourself the frustration. Ask for the obvious**.

Please note, though, having to ask for the obvious is in no way a reflection of how much other people care for you, or how much you mean to them. Most of us just aren't very good at anticipating what others need, especially when they are used to us not asking for support and taking care of everything ourselves.

Here is an opportunity for you to ask for the obvious. Whom would you ask, and what would you ask from them?

_____
_____
_____
_____
_____
_____
_____

Step 5: Accept Support

The next step to living a more empowered life is to accept the support you've been offered. In my experience, there are three main reasons why some people find it a challenge to accept support: a) they are overly independent, b) they have difficulty trusting others, or c) the support they receive looks different than they thought it would.

If you tend to do everything on your own, accepting offered support is a great opportunity for you to challenge your beliefs. Instead of responding with your usual, "No thanks, I've got it," **take the**

opportunity to accept support, even if you think you don't need it. Sometimes, very independent people become so entrenched in their current situations that they don't realize they need support or how it could help them. If this describes you, take the opportunity to challenge your beliefs and accept support when it is offered. Purposely change your "no" response to a "yes" when someone asks if they can offer you support, and then accept what will be most supportive to you. Practice with little things first until you create new behavior patterns.

Accepting support also requires trust, which can be a big hurdle for some. As I've previously discussed, trust of strangers may be an issue. Many of us have learned to rely on ourselves for so long that trusting someone with our hopes and dreams can be a big step, which makes accepting support pretty overwhelming.

If trust is an issue for you, take small steps and gradually increase the amount of support you ask for and accept from others. Not trusting someone to support you may be your instincts telling you that you are not asking the right person. Evaluate the situation and decide if there is an underlying belief causing the fear and mistrust or if your instincts are warning you of potential danger. Trust your instincts, while still challenging your beliefs. With each successful encounter, your support will gradually increase, and you'll feel more trusting, more energized, more liberated, and more powerful. Not trusting others may stem from not trusting our own instincts. Take it from someone who knows about not trusting. With time and practice, it is possible to trust yourself and others and create more support for yourself.

> **"Trust in yourself. Your perceptions are often far more accurate than you are willing to believe."**
> ∞ ***Claudia Black*** ∞

Finally, some people find it difficult to accept support because it doesn't look the way they envisioned it would. News flash: support doesn't always look the way you think it should. It's important to recognize when the Universe presents you with an opportunity. To make the most of that opportunity, you must be willing to accept that support for what it is. When support doesn't look the way you think it should, you may turn it away because of misperceptions of how valuable this form of support really is, but please be clear on your reason for turning it away. The thing is, support is support, and any help in moving forward could potentially be a welcome relief, if you are willing to accept it. Little opportunities that come your way, which you may think of as coincidences, may actually be covert pieces of support in your life.

In Step 3, I asked you to describe exactly the type of support you are looking for. In the space below, consider what support is currently available to you (even if it looks different from what you think it should), and whether or not you are willing to accept this support.

_____
_____
_____
_____
_____
_____

∞ What are your reasons for not accepting or trusting this support?

_____
_____
_____
_____
_____
_____

Step 6: Allow Support (From Other and Unexpected Sources)

Probably the most significant way to create more support in your life is to actually allow support into your life and to **be open to support from unexpected sources**. "Allowing" is different from "accepting." In *Law of Attraction*, Michael J. Losier defines allowing as experiencing "the absence of doubt." When we apply this definition to support, it means being fully open to the possibility that all the support you want and need is always there for you, exactly when you need it.

When we are fully open to the possibility of support, and have eliminated doubt and lack from our beliefs, we can learn to trust ourselves to always attract exactly the support we need. When we allow support into our lives, we ask for and accept support without any negative emotions attached to the outcome, knowing and trusting that we'll always get what we need.

Embracing Support

Meanwhile, Back at the Kingdom

One day the Prince and Princess were planning an evening out with some friends, the Duke and Duchess of Harris. Because her children mean the world to her, the Princess was very particular about who would look after the three- and six-year-old princesses, and she simply could not find a suitable babysitter that evening. In the end, she sent a telegram to the Duke to let him know she would have to take her kids along for the evening. He replied that his 12-year-old daughter had been babysitting for a while and had been doing an excellent job with 20-month-old twins. The Princess was reluctant to accept his help, and imagined all sorts of things that could go wrong with the situation and with the evening.

In the end, though, she decided she could trust her friend, whom she had known for more than 20 years. Although the Princess hadn't seen her friend's two children in many years, she knew she could trust him and his wife to have brought up their children to be capable and trustworthy. The Princess also decided this was a way in which the Universe could support her in creating a win-win situation for everyone. It was a new way to allow support.

They left all four kids (including the Duke's 10-year-old son) at the castle and went out for an amazing meal and a long-overdue visit. They had a wonderful evening, and the children had a ton of fun making new friends and playing games. The duke's daughter made 20 silver pieces for her babysitting work and was able to *come to the city for the day on an outing before babysitting in the evening. The Princess later thought, "That really was a win-win situation all around," simply because she was open to a form of support that didn't look the way she thought it should, and she was willing to allow this new support, knowing and trusting her instinct that everything was going to work out wonderfully.*

Inherent in all of this is that the Princess was clear on wanting support with her kids so she could go out for the evening, and she was willing to trust in a situation and in a friend. Through her openness to support looking different from what she thought it should, and accepting the support that was offered to her, everything turned out much better than she imagined.

It is human nature to resist change. **We tend to hold on to the old, more comfortable way of doing things because there is a certain safety in knowing the outcome of a situation.** Change can often create stress and fear. We may feel the need to prevent change and stay in what we consider our safe comfort zone. But as long as we hold on to our old ways, change can't truly happen. Change becomes a scary thing, and instead of being open to new ways of being, we repeat the same behaviors over and over and wonder why things never change.

In the case of support, we may reach out, ask for, and even accept support. But if we are not truly open to allowing support as a way of life, we will never fully receive all the support we want and need. By being open to a variety of sources of support—both sought

Embracing Support

out and spontaneously offered—we create subtle shifts in our beliefs that give us even greater opportunities, until support becomes a natural part of our life.

Now is an excellent time to consider: **what other sources of support are available to you that you're not allowing into your life?** Please note, these sources may be the ones addressed in Step 2, or they may be completely different sources that you have not yet considered.

_____
_____
_____
_____
_____
_____
_____
_____
_____
_____

∞ Who might be an additional source of support, or where could you access support that you haven't previously considered? Remember to think big.

_____
_____
_____
_____
_____
_____
_____
_____

> *"A man who really wants something will find a way; a man who doesn't will find an excuse."*
>
> ∞ **Unknown** ∞

Step 7: Celebrate Success with Gratitude

The final, and most overlooked step, is the celebration of success. Celebrating success creates new thoughts and emotions, which will help make asking and accepting support easier in the future. The truth is you can make having support as hard or as easy as you choose. There are literally thousands of people on the planet who are willing and able to support you. However, you have to ask first and then give them the opportunity to help. If you celebrate your success each time you receive the support you want and need, the whole process becomes easier and easier until it eventually becomes unconscious, and won't be a challenge for you anymore. Being consciously grateful for the support, and for your newfound ability to ask for, accept, and allow support builds new neuropathways that lead to new, unconscious behavior patterns.

Remember, seeking and accepting support is a process. It has taken you your entire life to get to where you are today. It makes sense that it will also take a little time to change your life. Celebrate each success and consciously make an effort to ask and receive support. Eventually it won't be a conscious effort anymore. It may even become a habit.

Celebrating success can be challenging in itself. How will you celebrate your success? What is one thing you can do to celebrate having taken the steps to ask for, accept, and allow support?

___

- What other ways can you think of to celebrate and show you are grateful for support from others?

___

Getting the Support You Want

By working through these steps you can look at any of your seven life areas and create more support within them. To reinforce the ideas presented in this chapter, there is an at-a-glance version of the exercise available on my website www.healwithsupport.com/resources that you can refer back to every time you want to be clear on the kind of support you want or need and how to get it.

So, What Have We Learned?

In this chapter:
- ✓ We've briefly reviewed what might be stopping you from having support by reflecting on beliefs that may still be in your way.
- ✓ We've challenged a few beliefs one more time.
- ✓ We've put strategies into action in seven easy steps:
  1. Know What You Want
  2. Find the Right Person
  3. Ask for Support (Act as If)
  4. Ask for the Obvious
  5. Accept Support
  6. Allow Support (From Other and Unexpected Sources)
  7. Celebrate Success with Gratitude

I hope you now feel as clear about how to get the support you need as I did when I learned these lessons. These amazing steps really do work, and the results you create will help you have your happy, empowered, amazing life with more support. All you need to do is ask, accept, and allow. With time and practice, asking for and accepting support will get easier for you, even if it doesn't seem that way now. Keep practicing and celebrate every time you ask, even if you didn't get what you were asking for.

"Dream as if you'll live forever, live as if you'll die today."

∞ ***James Dean*** ∞

Strategy 7: Take Care of Yourself (The Most Vital Support)

"I am not a product of my circumstances. I am a product of my decisions."
∞ **Stephen Covey** ∞

Meanwhile, Back at the Kingdom
The Princess was not well. She was tired, had trouble remembering things, and was sad a lot of the time. She cried for no apparent reason, or over meaningless things like breaking a bracelet or because a song reminded her of something. She wasn't sleeping well and was in physical pain. Her nights were spent tossing and turning, then she woke up tired, stiff, and sore from tension, and she started having headaches. She was overwhelmed by the smallest things and instead of using what little energy she had on short bursts of cleaning to eliminate some of the chaos from the castle renovations, she chose to instead play a game on her fancy new hand held communication device. But the more time she spent avoiding the clutter and turmoil, the worse her health became, and her relationships with her little princesses and the Prince became strained. She felt guilty for not cleaning and being preoccupied with her games. She had a huge argument with the Prince over the whole situation, and was now thinking about leaving the castle altogether and moving into a little

cottage closer to town, where there wouldn't be so much to deal with. She felt unhappy, lost, and taken for granted, and wanted a new start.

Then, late one night, the Princess came home from her work with the sick and dying and felt so low that she found herself sitting in her carriage, watching the night sky, contemplating if perhaps life was really worth living anymore. She was emotionally hurt and tired. Physically, her body ached from too much bending and lifting at work and from her poor sleep. She just wanted the pain to stop.

In tears, she looked at the beautiful night sky, with all the distant stars sparkling brightly, and she realized she had lost her purpose. All she was doing was running away from her problems, not actually solving them. She had been so busy "doing," that she forgot how to stop and just "be." In all the clutter, turmoil, and chaos of renovating the castle, and in avoiding her problems and relationships through playing games, she had lost her connection to the people she loved the most; the ones who supported her the best. And most of all, she had lost her connection to herself.

Allowing herself to reconnect with her own spirituality that night, she realized she had not been looking after herself. Although she told herself that playing her game was her down time, she realized this was simply a distraction. It was certainly not helping her regain inner peace and balance. So she sat, watching the stars, and allowed herself to grieve for her lost self. Finally feeling reconnected to the Universe, *her spirituality, and herself again, she went into the dark, quiet castle and started making a to-do list, just to get all the tumultuous thoughts out of her head. It was three pages long. But having it all written down meant her family could see it as well, and instead of wondering why nothing was getting done, they could all work on completing it together.*

The next day the family made a plan to better support each other. The Prince bought the Princess a new shelving unit with many shelves and drawers for her office so she had a better place to sort and store some of the papers and books she needed to keep, and in return, he received peace of mind because he could close the doors on the now-organized "stuff."

Then the Prince and the little princesses helped with cleaning the castle, and the family designated half an hour each day to work towards completing the list. Amazingly enough, with everyone working together, the long list was almost completed by the end of the month. There was less clutter and the Prince was able to come home to a cleaner home and have peace of mind, the Princess was able to make time to look after herself and participate in physical activities and socialize with her friends, and the little princesses had a cleaner, more peaceful place to play.

Everyone helped out with a few simple chores to complete when they came home, before they had play time in an organized play area. The laundry was sorted and put away, and overall the kingdom flourished financially

because less money was spent on items that weren't actually needed or were found in the clean-up. And the Princess? She now had time to engage in her creative activities, because her support system all worked together to get through the daily and weekly chores. Because she started looking after herself again, the Princess was able to HEAL her hurt emotions and lost connection to self, and asked the right people, for the right kind of support, at the right time.
And they finally lived happily ever after.

Up to this point, I have written mostly about how to ask for and accept support from others. In order to truly be supported, however, we also need to support ourselves. I call this "internal support." Internal support happens when we decide we are worthy of love and respect, and we treat ourselves the way we would like others to treat us. I have seen phenomenal changes in people who decide to love and honor themselves enough to create internal support. I have also seen it in myself.

How should we define internal support? If support is **a way to empower individuals to use the strength and love from others to create something miraculous for themselves**, then internal support is all the things you do for yourself to help you feel more loved, more productive, and more empowered. Internal support may mean taking the time to meditate or pray, exercise or do yoga, listen to music, sing, dance, go for a walk, spend time alone or with a loved one, visit a friend, change your mind or make a decision you've been putting off, do something creative, go for a massage, read a book—anything that helps you rejuvenate your heart and soul.

Interestingly, many of us are really great at supporting others, but not so good at supporting ourselves. As a nurse, I meet countless caregivers who are burnt out because they give and give to support others but do not look after themselves. The simple fact is, if you're not willing to support yourself by nurturing your body, mind, and soul, you will not be able to fully receive the support that others offer. Nor will you be able to give support to others without draining yourself in the process. In short, to be able to receive support from others, you first need to be able to support yourself.

Beliefs and Internal Support

I was an only child until almost age six. When my younger sister was born, my mom had periods of postpartum depression and, I later found out, intense fears about losing me to whatever horrible thing she thought of in the moment. Even though I don't have any concrete memories of these situations, I know that children are incredibly intuitive and learn quickly which actions and behaviors will get them more attention. Even more quickly than that, they decide to take on the beliefs of the adults in their lives and apply them to their current situations.

So, after my sister was born, I learned I received praise for being a "good girl" and I was valued for helping my mom look after my new baby sister and lending a hand around the house. This was the beginning of the belief, "I am valued and loved as long as I am doing something for someone"—a powerful belief that has affected the rest of my life. Until recently, I still found myself spending countless hours doing things for others, but never fully sure why I had agreed to help in the first place. Instead, I would become frustrated and resentful about sacrificing the things I truly wanted—like family time and "me" time.

This cycle perpetuated itself until I was burnt out completely. Unfortunately, my burnout coincided with my mom's cancer relapse. At a time when she needed me most, I was unable to be there for her. I felt guilty about what I "should" be doing for her, but I just couldn't help anymore. After caring for her for the four years since her initial diagnosis and stroke, and neglecting myself and my kids in the process, I finally set boundaries on what I was willing to do and how much time I was willing to spend with her. Although my timing sucked, these boundaries were the best thing I ever did for myself. Sadly, I had to experience an emotional and physical crisis before I learned that lesson.

The Next Generation

Because I'm now aware of the way my mom's beliefs affected me as a young girl, I pay closer attention to the words I use around my own kids. When my older daughter was about three and a half, she started helping me with her baby sister and with my ill mom. She received additional attention from me as I thanked her for being such a big help. I noticed we were perpetuating a cycle of praise and attention for the help she was giving. Then I caught myself. I realized I was recreating the circumstances I grew up in. Now we work on changing the belief, "I am valued and loved if I do something for someone else." I now reinforce how much I love and appreciate her, even when she is not doing something for me, and I consciously make an effort to spend time with her so she realizes that I love and value her for who she is, not for what she does. I'm happy to report she has grown into a perfectly normal, self-focused teenager.

Learning to Support Myself

The lesson I didn't learn as a child was that **I am valued for who I am, exactly as I am**. For whatever reason or circumstance, that belief didn't develop until much later in my life. I still catch myself sometimes agreeing to take on things for others that really aren't serving in my best interest. Looking back, I see how so many of my relationships (friends, boyfriends, family) were strained or doomed to fail from the start because I didn't value myself. I chose to surround myself with people who recreated these circumstances for me, and I was continually giving of myself or doing something for them so I could feel valued.

Being accountable, though, I don't blame my parents. Instead, I've learned to become aware of this trait and make new choices. I have finally learned to value and care for myself, and I am now working on expanding the context of how much I value myself to all areas of my life. I have learned to set boundaries with work, and I limit how much work interferes with family time or "me" time. If my students complain about not having their assignments back the minute they're handed in, I explain my limited work hours and my responsibilities. The important thing is to explain the boundary, not make excuses. I let them know why marking their papers takes time and that it's not the end of the world if they don't get their papers back as quickly as they'd hoped, and they usually respect me for setting that boundary. When I'm being true to myself, supporting myself, and setting boundaries with work and my students, I am also setting an example for the next generation of nurses on how important internal support is, especially for caregivers.

There are other ways in which I support myself. In addition to making time to read, write, play, swim, be physically active, go for massages, and spend time with my family, I also set boundaries around my other job. If the staffing office calls me to work a shift at the hospital, I consciously decide whether I want to go or not, based on what else I have planned, never because I need the money. I stopped working only for money almost 20 years ago. That's when I decided I would only work if I enjoyed the work. About 90% of the time I make that happen by choosing my attitude about work. I've been working as a nursing instructor for almost 20 years, and I've been a Registered Nurse for almost 25. I still love both of my jobs. As soon as work feels like something I *have* to do, I either change how often I go to work, or I change my attitude about it. It's that simple. By making that choice consciously, I empower myself. And after all, I agreed to the contract or to work the shift. So, I will *choose* to make the most of it.

Setting Priorities

It's not just caregivers who need to look after

themselves. All of us have many responsibilities in our day, and sometimes we agree to take on too much. The most important thing you can do for yourself is to always make internal support (looking after yourself) a priority. This may mean asking for external support (from others) first, so you can make time for internal support. If we make a conscious effort to support ourselves first, we can learn, over time, to set boundaries around how much we're willing to take on. Unfortunately, we usually sacrifice internal support when external pressures pile up. How often have you sacrificed working out, having quiet alone time, or even eating lunch because something more pressing came along?

Until I learn to put myself first 100% of the time, I will continue to ask for external support to get me where I need to be. I'm still a work in progress, and putting myself first does take practice. However, like anything else, internal support gets easier over time and eventually turns into unconscious choices and behaviors. Like building muscle, **repetition and practice are required**.

In instances when I yet again underestimate the amount of time I need for work, and work starts piling up, I negotiate with my husband or in-laws to look after the kids for a weekend, so I can take some extra time to catch up on things. This often happens to me towards the end of the school term, when papers need to be marked, exams need to be developed and graded, and deadlines for final marks are looming. I know this is the nature of my job, and my husband and I work around this four-week period, knowing that after this stressful time is over, I will be able to catch up on things left undone at home, because I'll have a few weeks off. When I have free time again, I'll return the favor, so he can go sledding, quadding, or do some other outdoor physical or male bonding activity with his friends for a weekend. We negotiate and stick to the agreement. In a roundabout way, this too is internal support. Because my husband's support allows me to get caught up at work or at home, the pressure is off and I can focus on living again.

Lately, I've even begun to set boundaries around how many courses I'm willing to teach, consciously choosing how many hours I'm willing to work, based on the time commitment each will take. Likewise, when the hospital calls for me to pick up extra shifts, I consciously choose if I want to work the extra hours. If I decide this is my time off, I will not let myself be guilted into working extra shifts. This is a conscious financial decision I have made because I've decided that, for me to stay healthy, I will not work at a full-time position while my kids are still in school, I will not get involved in workplace politics, and I will not let myself get burnt out from constant and demanding work expectations. This is how internal support works for me. These boundaries allow me to be passionate about the work I do, which in turn allows me to be an inspiration to those I work with because I'm usually happy and love what I do. The minute this doesn't happen anymore, I change my work hours, or my attitude about what I choose to accept as work hours.

Financially, my decisions about work mean I choose to spend a bit less. Sometimes, I consciously choose to work extra hours if I want some extra income. Realistically, there are many things I spend money on that are not necessities; things I am willing to forgo or to buy second-hand. When I go shopping with my kids and they ask me for something I'm not willing to buy, I am honest with them. I tell them I'm not *willing* to spend money on that particular item, or I'm not *willing* to spend that amount. I never say I can't afford it, because in all honesty, if I wanted to spend that money, I probably could. Not because I have it, but because I would find a way.

A Reflection about Scarcity and Abundance

I realize I'm quite fortunate in my financial circumstances, and I worked very hard to get here. Yet even as a student putting myself through school, I never went without. There were times when I worked three and four jobs and still barely got by, but I always managed because of the way I look at money. Although my mom's fears about scarcity affected my beliefs about abundance in the Universe, I have also learned there is vast abundance for those of us who choose to look for it and accept it. Acting as if I am safe and secure in my finances, decreasing limiting beliefs about scarcity, and being conscious of how I spend my income have given me a sense of freedom and empowerment for a long time. Most importantly, I love and respect myself enough to say no to work when it does not serve me or would drain my energy.

"There is no scarcity of opportunity to make a living at what you love; there's only scarcity of resolve to make it happen."
∞ *Dr. Wayne Dyer* ∞

Calling all Caregivers

I want to take a moment to address all the caregivers out there. I want you to consider how often you selflessly give of yourself, sometimes to your own detriment and illness, so your children or loved ones can have the best. In particular, I want you to think about the times you've decided to put off your play (social life, hobbies, etc.) or work (paid work, house work, schoolwork, any work at all), in order to spend time with your kids, friends, or family requiring your support. Maybe you skip breakfast or arrive late at work so you can walk the kids to school. Or maybe you decide to work or study in the evening after the kids are in bed so you can spend time with them when they are awake. Or you miss a meal or sleep because you're helping a friend or visiting someone in the hospital. How much do we sacrifice for our kids or the people we care for? When I think about the number of times I've decided to leave my work or something I wanted to do for myself to spend time with my kids, I tell myself I do it because I want them to have the best of everything; I do it for them.

However, kids (and the people we care for) can tell when we caregivers are fully present for them and when we're not. The truth is, when my kids were little, they didn't enjoy my company when I did give it to them, because they knew I was thinking about work or my other to-do list. They want to spend quality time with me—not time when I'm tired or distracted. They liked the stuff I bought them, but in all reality, they'd rather have less stuff and more of their mom. All they ever wanted from me was for me to play with them, and the best way for me to do this was to care for and

Embracing Support

rejuvenate myself. Then we could do things together and I could be fully present. Or better yet, we could do things together that rejuvenated us all.

As a parent, as a caregiver, or just as a caring person, how many times do we feel guilty about taking time to look after and support ourselves? For example, I may decide to have a calm, soothing bath to rejuvenate, but because I feel like I need to give to my kids and husband first, I will spend my time with them or doing something for them and then have my bath late in the evening after everyone's gone to bed. In the end, I sacrifice sleep in exchange for that bath. Great way to support myself.

I encourage those of you who sacrifice your own well-being in order to care for others to stop the cycle. As children we are taught not to be selfish and that it's better to give than to receive. The truth of the matter is, the more we are willing to give to ourselves, and the more internal support we create, the happier and stronger and more loving we are, which then leads to having more to give to others, should we decide to do so. Taking time to rejuvenate our body, mind, and soul affects every aspect of life. We feel stronger physically, we feel more enlightened mentally, we feel happier and more emotionally stable, we feel more connected spiritually, we feel safer in our environment and more satisfied financially, and we feel more open socially.

"Sharpening the Saw"

I hope at this point you understand the value of internal support, but let's make sure we're all clear and on the same page. In *The 7 Habits of Highly Effective*

People, Steven Covey refers to taking the time to care for yourself as filling your "emotional bank account" and that in order to be truly effective we need to "sharpen the saw." Essentially, he is saying we have to look after ourselves first, in all areas of our lives, in order to be more effective in what we do. If we stop long enough to "sharpen the saw" or rejuvenate ourselves, we will be more effective and more productive, and be able to get that much closer to living a loving and fulfilling life. It takes much longer to cut down a tree with a dull saw.

It isn't always easy to keep an eye on your emotional bank account, though. Sometimes it's when we most need to take care of ourselves that we don't. When I find myself under time pressures, I often neglect looking after myself. I'll book a massage, but then find myself debating if I should cancel the appointment so I can get caught up on other tasks instead. The thing is, taking that hour out of my busyness to look after myself can make a world of difference in my energy level and clarity of thinking. I bring more joy to my work, making it easier to complete. I'm much more focused and get things done faster, I have more energy to play with my kids, I feel more loving towards my husband, and I feel like I can ask for more support from others. I have to be willing to support myself first though. When I'm working with a "dull saw," everything takes that much longer. By not stopping to sharpen it, I'm contributing to the problem. Once I finally do take care of myself, everything comes together beautifully.

Embracing Support

Mix It Up!

Sometimes, taking time for yourself is simply a matter of listening to your inner voice and following your instincts. For example, I like to keep moving; I have a tough time sitting still for any length of time. I'm sure this ties into my beliefs about being valued for what I do, and it's also difficult for me to just "be." Yet when I don't really feel like doing something, I can be a huge procrastinator. When it comes to procrastination, I am a genius. I have all the reasons and excuses in the world for not getting stuff done. My favorite form of procrastination, interestingly enough, is cleaning. My house is never as clean as when I have papers to mark. That's when even the clutter gets cleaned up. My husband will come home to me cleaning out the pantry or the freezer and ask me what it is I'm avoiding. But I digress . . .

The morning of the day I had set aside time to work on this last portion of the book, I woke up with a headache and just felt *blah*. I turned on my computer, planning to listen to some quiet music to get me in the mood to write. As it happened, I clicked on the wrong song, and some upbeat music came pouring out of my speakers. Well, that was that. I turned it up, and instead of sitting down and writing for a few hours like I promised myself, I started cleaning and moving and dancing to the music.

I tidied up the clutter on my kitchen counters, I scrubbed cookie sheets, I cleaned off parts of my desk, and I reorganized my work bag. After about an hour, I caught myself and asked, "What are you doing? You have writing to get done." As it turns out, by allowing myself to get swept up in the moment, I was actually supporting myself. I hadn't been looking forward to sitting for four hours and struggling with words that wouldn't come. By doing something physical, which I really needed to do to reset my brain, I was doing something for myself. I enjoyed the singing and dancing, and I was then able to sit down and write for six hours straight. I finished this segment in one day. By supporting myself and giving myself permission to do some physical activity, I was able to write with passion. Little things like this make a big difference in feeling more love and empowerment of self.

A Reflection about Procrastination

It's important to be clear about what you're doing for internal support and the activities you participate in. Are you going for a run or taking a bath as a form of internal support or simply to avoid doing something else? Do your actions truly support you to create something positive? Procrastination and internal support have two very different outcomes. Having clear intentions on the purpose of the activity will help you distinguish between the two.

"Taking care of yourself makes you stronger for everyone in your life . . . including you."
∞ **Kelly Rudolph** ∞

The Seven Domains of Internal Support

Most types of internal support fall into one of seven domains: physical, intellectual/mental, emotional, spiritual, financial/occupational, environmental, or social. You may be familiar with these areas, as much of the published information available to us also divides personal wellness into these six to eight categories (depending on the source). For the purpose of this section, I've chosen seven main domains. To help you evaluate the state of your own internal support, I've provided an outline of each of these domains and asked you to reflect on what you are currently doing to support yourself in each area.

As you learn about the Seven Domains of Internal Support, keep in mind there is a great deal of overlap between them. The goal of this activity is to look at what you currently have or do in each domain and then look at increasing internal support where it may be lacking, so you can create balance for yourself. If you are not currently supporting yourself in one or more domains, you'll know where to create more internal support for yourself. The goal is a moderate and balanced array of internal support. Remember, the key to balance is "everything in moderation."

The Physical Domain of Internal Support

When you support yourself in the physical domain, you contribute to or improve your physical body and health or well-being, which includes your overall quality of life and how well you manage your daily tasks (a.k.a. activities of daily living). Physical activity such as regularly moving your body, increasing your heart rate or strengthening muscles (such as through running, walking, dancing, swimming, going to the gym, yoga, strengthening, or moving your body in any other way) is one aspect of this domain, but it also includes the way you interact with the physical environment in which you live and work. For example, how you respond to workplace or neighborhood noise or your level of stress has an impact on your physiology and your physical and mental well-being. The physical domain is varied and also includes adequate amounts of sleep, physical and sexual intimacy and safety, and eating healthy and nutritious meals at regular intervals, just to name a few. Additionally, the decisions you make about your health—informing yourself about healthy lifestyle choices, acting on these, and seeking medical attention when necessary—are also an important aspect of your physical health.

The physical domain is the main area where I'm not yet internally supporting myself (or asking for external support for that matter), primarily when it comes to looking after my body. I've told you about my weight issues, and in reality I'm okay with the weight I am. However, I know I would feel so much better about myself and about life in general if I chose to treat my body with the love and respect it deserves, by making better choices about what I eat, how I move my body, and how much sleep I get each night. Looking after my body more effectively would help me manage my stress better, and have an overall more peaceful life experience.

Embracing Support

Here are a few questions you can ask yourself to discover whether or not you are supporting yourself in the physical domain:
- ∞ Are you a healthy weight for your height?
- ∞ Do you drink enough water to promote healthy body and brain function?
- ∞ How much exercise do you participate in?
- ∞ Did that just trigger a belief? How about if I ask, "How often do you move your body to either increase your heart rate or strengthen your muscles?"
- ∞ Do you get seven or eight hours of uninterrupted sleep at night? Do you wake up rested?
- ∞ Do you have physical intimacy in your life?
- ∞ Are you content to spend time with yourself?
- ∞ Do you consume an adequate amount of healthy calories from nutritious foods and limit your intake of sugar, caffeine, and other substances that affect healthy body function?
- ∞ Do you regularly eat too much or too little?
- ∞ Do you use other chemicals that can have an effect on your physical body such as alcohol, tobacco, street drugs (legal or illegal), or medications that are not used for what they're intended? What about your shampoo, body lotion, perfume, hair products or other chemicals you're regularly exposed to?
- ∞ How are your blood pressure and cholesterol levels?
- ∞ How much stress do you experience at work? At home?
- ∞ Do you experience physical pain? What impact

does it have on your daily activities? How do you manage the pain?
∞ Are you able to maintain a healthy quality of life?
∞ Are you able to complete your daily activities without excessive physical stress or tiredness?

Questions such as these will help you become clearer on the level of physical internal support you currently have. Although many of these areas have intellectual/mental, emotional, social, and even environmental implications as well, stress, and fear in particular have a big physical impact on your immune system and on your metabolism, just as the use of alcohol, tobacco, drugs and other chemicals does.

As you consider the above questions, turn to the Seven Domains of Internal Support Diagram on the next page and take a few minutes to write down in the physical domain circle the types of physical internal support that you currently engage in and, if applicable, how often. By completing this diagram, you'll have a clearer overview of which areas you have an abundance of internal support, and where you have less. Use that information to focus on your internal support needs and then ask for external support. If you'd like a printable version of this diagram, you can access it on my website www.healwithsupport.com/resources.

Embracing Support

The Seven Domains of Internal Support Diagram

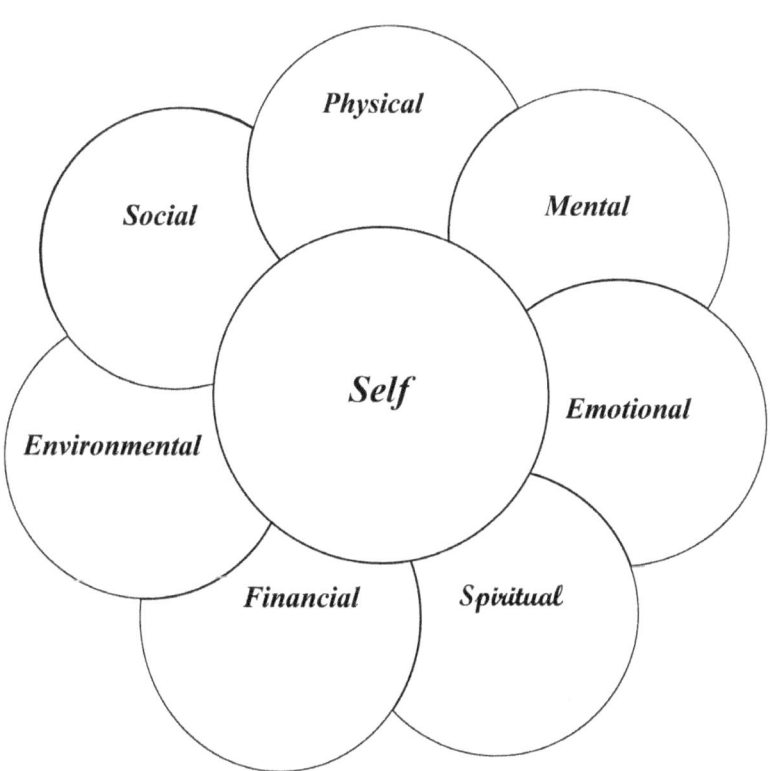

The Intellectual/Mental Domain of Internal Support

When you support yourself in the intellectual or mental domain of internal support, you stimulate your mind, challenge your intellect, reduce your stress, and make intelligent, informed decisions based on what you have learned from past experiences. Together, this benefits your overall health and well-being. This might include learning something new, challenging yourself to a new skill or language, challenging yourself to be creative (even if you say you're not), playing games of strategy (such as chess) or problem-solving games or activities, or building or teaching something new. You're also able to be open-minded and critically think about new experiences or ideas to expand your own beliefs and values. Working at a job that stimulates your mind as well as thinking about how newly learned information affects your health, your environment, and the betterment of your community can also fit into this domain.

If you do not challenge yourself intellectually, you may find yourself bored with life or feel stuck in a rut. You may be uninterested at work or sit in front of the TV or computer at home, mindlessly letting information wash over you. Additionally, if you experience high levels of stress or fear, or an imbalance between work and family time or self time, these will play havoc with your body, affecting both your immune system and your metabolism.

In today's electronic age, we tend to be glued to our devices, which are filled with games and other distractions, and sometimes we think the games we play are intellectually or mentally challenging us

Embracing Support

because there is a problem-solving component involved. I challenge you to critically consider whether these games truly stimulate your intellect, or if your time could be spent on more challenging activities. Also consider how much time you're spending on your devices, and think about activities you could be doing instead that will challenge your intellect and get you more involved in your environment and community.

Here are a few questions you can ask yourself to discover whether or not you are supporting your intellectual/mental well-being:

- ∞ Do you take time to be creative, for example, by writing, painting, reading, sewing, playing an instrument, or taking pictures of something beautiful?
  - o Hint: If your answer is, "I'm not creative," here's a great place to increase your internal support in the intellectual domain by challenging that belief and purposely doing something creative. Change your thought pattern to, "I haven't learned to be creative yet," and then pick something . . . anything. You may surprise yourself.
- ∞ Do you challenge the beliefs that you developed in the past?
- ∞ Do you consciously make choices that take you outside your comfort zone?
- ∞ Do you make an effort to change the words you use in your everyday language to create a more supportive life for yourself?
- ∞ Are you taking steps to manage stress in your life?
- ∞ Do you pay attention to your surroundings and

try to see something new every day?
- Do you take conscious steps to live outside your routine?
- Do you make an effort to get to know someone or something new every day?
- Do you consciously challenge unconscious habits?
- Do you willingly change your routine, just to "mix it up"?
- Do you engage in intellectual conversations that challenge your views?
- Are you open to new ideas and different perspectives?
- Do you critically think about past experiences and how you have learned new information that you can apply to your life, health, and well-being?
- Do you have a balance between work, family, and leisure time?

Intellectual/mental and physical internal support activities sometimes overlap. For example, if you're playing a sport that requires thought, learning new dance or martial arts moves, or doing aerobics, both your physical and mental capacities are required.

Now return to the Seven Domains of Internal Support Diagram and take a few minutes to write down the types of intellectual/mental internal support you currently participate in and, if applicable, how often.

Embracing Support

> *"Everyone and everything that shows up in our life is a reflection of something that is happening inside of us."*
> ∞ *Alan Cohen* ∞

The Emotional Domain of Internal Support

When you support yourself in the emotional domain, you strengthen your ability to understand yourself and the emotions you're experiencing, you're able to express your emotions, and you can recognize your strengths and limitations. In other words, you accept who you are emotionally. If you're an emotionally well-adapted person, you are able to not just control your emotions, but also handle experiencing and expressing them appropriately. Then you're able to communicate your emotions effectively, and ask for support when you need it. If you're feeling sad, it's okay to cry. If you're angry, it's okay to express that anger in a healthy way. For example, when my youngest daughter was five, I taught her it's okay to say, "I'm mad!" instead of clenching her fists and screaming. On the other hand, sometimes you just need to scream. It's *how* you express yourself that's important, and the fact that you do express yourself instead of internalizing or "stuffing" your emotions.

In *You Can Heal Your Life*, Louise Hay stresses that emotions need to "move" because if they just sit, they can fester and create illness. From a medical perspective I can tell you how important it is to our mental health to be able to express our emotions. It's important that you find creative ways to express yourself at work, at home, and with friends and family to help "move" your emotions.

Sometimes, gossiping can be a way to express emotions, but I caution you about this approach. If you tend to gossip, I encourage you to think about your message, and have a look at your beliefs about yourself, your job, others, and your life that may show up in your complaints.

Some supportive ways of expressing emotions include singing, dancing, running, kicking, swimming, screaming, painting, drawing, gardening, doing a physical activity that requires strength, working out, watching a sad movie to help you cry or a funny one to get you laughing, writing poetry or a story, and writing your thoughts in a journal. My personal favorite is taking out my frustrations on the heavy bag I have in my basement, and in serious cases, I clean my house (scrubbing floors or throwing things out). Do you see how often emotional internal support takes the form of physical activity?

Here are a few questions you can ask yourself to discover whether or not you are supporting your emotional well-being:

- ∞ How do you feel about showing emotions to others, or having others be emotional in your presence? Are some emotions more comfortable to express or be around than others?
- ∞ When you see others expressing emotions such as joy, pain, sadness, or love, can you empathize with what they're feeling and/or be supportive? Are some emotions easier to be empathetic with than others?
- ∞ How do you express your own emotions (do

you pick one or run through the list)?
- ∞ When something upsetting or stressful happens, what is your default emotion?
- ∞ When was the last time you cried? What was the reason?
- ∞ How do you deal with anger?
- ∞ What makes you laugh?
- ∞ When you are sad or upset, how do others know?
- ∞ Hint: If your answer is "they don't," consider the reason for this.
- ∞ How do you react when someone hurts your feelings?
- ∞ How often do you laugh throughout the day? What makes you smile?
- ∞ What did you learn about how to express emotions while you were growing up? How were emotions expressed in your home?
- ∞ What was the most prevalent emotion expressed while you were growing up? What about now?
- ∞ What do you do when you feel emotionally stuck?

Now return to the Seven Domains of Internal Support Diagram and take a few minutes to write down the types of emotional internal support you currently participate in and, if applicable, how often.

"Emotions are natural, like passing weather. Sometimes it's fear, sometimes sorrow or anger. Emotions are not the problem. The key

is to transform the energy of emotion into constructive action."
∞ **Socrates** ∞
The Peaceful Warrior (Film)

The Spiritual Domain of Internal Support

When you support yourself in the spiritual domain, you create and maintain love, hope, peace, tranquility, purpose, and a connection to the Universe or a belief in something greater than yourself, whether that is through God, creator, spirit, Universe, or another source (insert your own belief here). However, the spiritual domain also includes understanding your personal beliefs, values, and ethics, and being happy with how you conduct your life. As with any form of internal support, there may be overlap with other areas, as there is a great range of ways that you can nurture your spirituality, because each of us defines spirituality in our own way. To me, spirituality encompasses my connection with myself, others, and the world in general in how I treat others and live my life. It's about living life with love and purpose, gratitude and generosity, and giving back as much as I receive. Spending time connected to others is just as much a part of spirituality as spending time alone and reflecting on life and the world around me.

Creating spiritual internal support might include practicing an attitude of gratitude for all we have, going to church, praying, living our lives by our own ethical principles, singing, listening to music, meditating, doing yoga, drawing or painting, journal writing, gardening, cleaning, donating time or money, helping others, or spending time in nature. But it also means much more. Spiritual internal support includes creating meaning, living our life's purpose, being enlightened, being an inspiration to others, promoting love for all life, and leaving behind a legacy. Taking the time to create something that symbolizes your connection to self, others, and the Universe, or doing a selfless deed may be a powerful way to nurture your internal support.

Spiritual internal support can be a challenging domain, partly because many people equate spirituality with religion. However, it's important to understand that these are two very different things. Organized religion is merely one form of expressing spirituality. Whether people do or don't believe in organized religion, everyone needs to nurture their spiritual selves and think about how they conduct their lives and what their higher purpose in life is. When people don't feel like they have a purpose in life, it may be difficult for them to feel a connection to love, to life, or to the Universe. If you find you do little in the way of spiritual internal support, I encourage you to spend some time looking at your beliefs about spirituality and/or religion. Please don't limit yourself by equating spirituality only with religion.

To find balance and love in my life, I go for walks and take pictures of nature. I fill my emotional bank account by taking quiet time to reflect and read books I enjoy. I've discovered I like working in the garden and watching things grow. To me, spirituality is about inspiration, love, and hope, and I get inspired through creating and writing. I live my life with love of self and others, and foster interconnectedness with others. I believe we all have a purpose and that everything that happens in our lives has a meaning and a reason. I believe my job is to discover that purpose, learn from it, inspire others, and practice gratitude for the experience.

Here are a few questions you can ask yourself to discover whether or not you are supporting your spiritual well-being:
- ∞ What is your definition of spirituality?
- ∞ How do you distinguish or differentiate between spirituality and religion?
- ∞ Do you resist participating in conversations that have to do with spirituality? Do these conversations make you feel uncomfortable?
- ∞ Are your beliefs about spirituality and religion *your* beliefs, or are they the ones you learned from your parents or someone else while you were growing up?
- ∞ Are your beliefs today the same as those you learned as a child? If yes, are these beliefs still true for you today?
- ∞ How do you think spirituality can have an overall impact on your health and well-being?
- ∞ Do you feel connected to the rest of humanity and to existence in the Universe in general?
- ∞ Do you practice gratitude for all you have or all you could have if you chose to access it?
- ∞ How do you create or maintain hope? Love? Peace? Tranquility?
- ∞ Do you have peace in your life? If not, how could you create this with love?
- ∞ How would you help someone else find their connection to spirituality?
- ∞ What are your own beliefs and values about

life, love and the world around you?

∞ Do you live your life in an ethical way?

Now return to the Seven Domains of Internal Support Diagram and take a few minutes to write down what you currently do to create balance, love, interconnectedness, hope, peace, purpose, and tranquility in your life and, if applicable, how often.

"A mind at peace, a mind centered and not focused on harming others is stronger than any physical force in the universe."
∞ *Dr. Wayne Dyer* ∞

The Financial/Occupational Domain of Internal Support

When you support yourself in the financial/occupational domain, you create a state of mind that allows you to feel safe about and in control of your financial situation. This might include working at a job you enjoy, choosing to work where you feel your time is suitably compensated, feeling appreciated for your contributions, and having a certain level of job security. Feeling safe financially can also include setting up your banking so money is automatically transferred into savings accounts before you get the chance to spend it, creating educational savings accounts for your children, maximizing access to government grants, setting aside money for house repairs and new appliances, and/or starting a travel/vacation fund. Additionally, paying off your credit card bill each month, choosing not to buy on impulse, consciously deciding to purchase based on worth, value, and need rather than want are some other ways you can create financial security. Being open to receiving money, finding money and free things, and celebrating each gift received are just as important as spending money on self with moderation, choosing where and how often to work, and changing fears about lack of money and scarcity to thoughts of abundance. Feeling grateful for the income you do have and for your capabilities to create more income are another way to feel financially secure. Additionally, look at how well you manage job-related stress and work-life balance, how well you get along with your co-workers and supervisors, and your ability to grow professionally. Consider your beliefs about your own ability to find or create a meaningful occupation and/or income.

Financial internal support may be challenging, depending on your beliefs about money. If you believe you do not have enough money in your life, or that there is not enough money in the world in general, you may continue to find yourself lacking in this area. If this is your belief, I challenge you to create internal support by striving to achieve balance in your finances and in your beliefs about finances (ask for support if need be). Feeling safe about your finances is a large part of creating that balance. I also challenge you to start seeing and thinking about abundance in any form. Take a look around. Where do you see abundance? Now know that you can also create that for yourself. You have the capability.

Because we rely on others for our income (whether as employees who are paid for our time or as business owners who rely on customer demand) and thus lack complete control over our finances, income is often associated with ideas of self-worth. This common belief affects the way many people think about money, but in reality, the two have nothing to do with each other. **What you as an individual are worth has nothing to do with what you get paid for your time at work.** If you can separate these two ideas, you're a big step closer to creating financial and occupational internal support.

In order to create balance in this area, you need to recognize what your own beliefs are about money and your self-worth, but you also need to take control and make powerful choices. If you recall, there are only three things we truly have control over: our thoughts, our behaviors, and our emotions or feelings. We can't necessarily control what an employer is willing to pay us, but we can decide to accept or reject an employer's offer for money in exchange for our time. We can control how we feel about that amount of money and how it reflects on our self-worth. Additionally, we can control how we spend our earnings.

Here are a few questions you can ask yourself to discover whether or not you are supporting your financial well-being:

- ∞ What are your current beliefs about money? Are these your own beliefs or those you decided to accept from others?
- ∞ How do you feel about discussing your finances with others?
- ∞ What support could you access to help you become more financially stable?
- ∞ How do you define financial freedom?
- ∞ What are you grateful for financially? (e.g.,

having a job, being able to work, having income, being able to afford life's necessities, etc.)
- ∞ If you were to write down all your complaints about your finances, what would these statements sound like? What if you were to change them to accountable language using "I choose" statements? (This is how you can take control over each statement, and shift the balance of power.)
  - o Hint: if you're not happy with your finances or occupation (or any other of the seven life areas), create a Contrast List and start focusing on what you really do want.
- ∞ What can you do to create financial or occupational internal support and balance?
- ∞ What did you learn about money growing up? What stories did you hear about money as a child?
- ∞ Do you have a budget or plan on how to spend your money or do you spend it as necessities come up?
- ∞ Who is in control of your spending?
- ∞ What options do you have to make more money? To spend less?
- ∞ Do you have a "rainy day" fund in case of emergencies?
- ∞ Do you feel valued and/or appreciated at the place where you earn your income?
- ∞ Do you agree with your employer's perception of what your time is worth?
- ∞ If there's one thing you would like to change about your job, what would it be? Is it within

your control to make that change?

Now return to the Seven Domains of Internal Support Diagram and take a few minutes to write down what you currently do to contribute to financial and occupational balance in your life and, if applicable, how often.

The Environmental Domain of Internal Support

When you support yourself in the environmental domain, you contribute to or improve your immediate surroundings, as well as the world you live in. **Our relationship with our environment and our ability to have an impact on its quality** is one part of this domain. Making conscious choices to walk, bike, or use public transportation instead of driving; engaging in recycling and using environmentally friendly products that produce less chemicals or garbage; or taking responsibility for the air and water quality and the land around us all affect our level of internal support. They are just as important as creating a safe home environment with enough lighting to protect our eye sight, protecting our hearing by reducing loud noises, and taking overall responsibility for the spaces we work, play and live in. If you experience a lot of clutter, or are overly stimulated by continual noise or interruptions, this will affect your overall health and well-being.

It's no accident that I'm writing this section while we are in the midst of renovations. All my younger daughter's furniture and belongings are parked in my office because we're painting her room and cleaning the carpets. There is a small path between the clutter from the office entrance to my desk. I'm finding it exceedingly difficult to form these thoughts as I sit surrounded by this huge pile of stuff. I also didn't sleep well last night, knowing there is so much stuff piled up, waiting to be dealt with. Thus, I encourage you to consider the space you live in as part of internal support. Decluttering your bedroom and increasing airflow will improve your sleep. Creating a clean space where you spend most of your waking time at home (for example your kitchen or living room) will allow you to feel more at peace. Decreasing the amount of "stuff" in your home will help you feel lighter and freer. Complete priority projects on your list by focusing on one at a time, and then shorten your mental (or written) to-do list. This will result in a new mental calm, create more energy, and allow you to *be* rather than do. (I've included an organizational tool, found in the resources section on my website www.healwithsupport.com/resources, which has been very beneficial for me to cut down on my clutter and prioritize my to-do list. Give it a try to see if you find it helpful.)

    I do what I can to be conscientious about the resources I use as my small contribution to saving the planet. I limit how much power we use; I print as little as possible and usually multiple pages per sheet to reduce paper use, and use both sides of the paper; I take cardboard and plastic bottles home with me from holidays to recycle at home if there's no recycling opportunity where I'm at; and in general I have a reusable water bottle and tea mug I carry with me. As a society we have become so used to throwaway items that we forget the greater impact we have on our environment. I encourage you to create internal support in this domain by consciously looking at your environment (your home, your work, and our planet in general) and taking steps to also consciously reduce, reuse and recycle. Using second-hand items or selling items I no longer need, donating to families in need, and using reusable containers for lunches is just one small part we can all participate in to make a big impact on the amount of garbage we produce. We can each do our part for the grander care and responsibility for our world.

Here are a few questions you can ask yourself to discover whether or not you work, play, and live in a supportive environment:

- ∞ Do you live in a noisy neighborhood where relaxation and sleep can be challenging?
- ∞ What is the air quality like where you play, live, and work?
- ∞ How much clutter is there in your home?
  - o Hint: let's define clutter as anything that doesn't have a permanent home in a cupboard, closet, or neatly organized shelf, and is laying around where it does not belong, gets shuffled around, or is in the way.
- ∞ What purpose does the "stuff" in your environment serve? Do you use it regularly or do you keep it because it has sentimental value?
- ∞ What emotions do you experience when you think about throwing out or giving away excess "stuff"?
- ∞ What can you do to reduce the amount of

"stuff" in your space?
- ∞ If you struggle with letting go of "stuff," what support could you access to help you with this process?
- ∞ How would you feel in a clean, clutter-free space?
- ∞ Is there a possibility of reorganizing anything within your home or work space (e.g. new or different shelving or storage units)?
- ∞ Do you actively participate in minimizing how much garbage you produce and how much you are able to recycle?
- ∞ Do you have access to a green space, have plants in your home, or are you able to enjoy interactions with nature?
- ∞ When you step out of your home, are you safe in your travels to where you're going?
- ∞ When considering the environment you live, play, and work in, are you afraid of anything in your daily life?

Now return to the Seven Domains of Internal Support Diagram and take a few minutes to write down the types of environmental internal support you currently participate in and, if applicable, how often.

"We have not inherited this earth from our parents to do with it what we will.
We have borrowed it from our children and we must be careful to use it in their interests as well as our own."
∞ ***Moses Henry Cass*** ∞
Australian Minister for the Environment and Conservation

The Social Domain of Internal Support

When you support yourself in the social domain, you increase your sense of self-worth through contact with others or through self-reflection. Supporting yourself in this area includes joining a peer support group, visiting close friends, attending a personal development course (which can also support your intellectual/mental and emotional domains), getting to know your neighbors and co-workers, taking a risk by talking to a stranger on the street, or spending more time with your family. Activities such as chatting and emailing, writing letters to distant relatives, or establishing connections with others, and challenging yourself to take a risk and challenge your beliefs about trust also contribute to social internal support. It's both about having a strong social network of support that is tolerant and accepting of each other, especially if you're stressed or not feeling well, and about setting boundaries and decreasing the amount of social interaction you have when it interferes with other areas of internal support. It's about developing healthy, supportive relationships, being able to relate and connect with others, feeling like you're part of a community, being tolerant of others, and forming close, empathic, and loving relationships where you feel safe to be yourself, and where you can effectively communicate with others. Remember that you want to achieve balance, and that may mean handing off responsibilities to others or delegating. Social internal support also includes finding peace and tranquility and being okay spending time by yourself.

For example, I was never one for socializing. I was always too busy. I didn't have time to just sit around, idly wasting time with useless conversation—which was my perception of social interaction. At least, that's what I told myself. In reality, I felt awkward in social conversations, and I didn't want to let people get close to me because I often felt judged and I didn't trust them not to hurt me when they left. As you've probably guessed, this attitude was directly linked to my beliefs. Once I made the connection about how my beliefs affected how I socialized with others, and consciously worked on those beliefs, socializing actually became easier and a source of support. However, no sooner did I finally become more comfortable in socializing and in drawing support from others, my life changed in an interesting way. After I had finally learned to let people in and started establishing new, closer relationships, I lost my mom and six of my new close friends moved away. Talk about challenging my beliefs. After having finally learned to establish supportive relationships and trusting these individuals, I got to start all over. But this time, I had the skills to build new relationships, so I got to work making new, supportive connections.

The interesting thing is, as I've been working on changing my beliefs, I realized that even though I'm going to miss these people terribly, I'm also going to be okay. New relationships will fill some of these gaps. I'm learning it's safe to be who I am, and I'm learning to be more open with people and sharing of myself without feeling judged about what they may see lacking in me. **I am good enough just as I am, and I am loved for who I am**. Look at everything I've shared with you so far. It wasn't easy putting all of that on paper.

Alternatively, I have a co-worker who just loves to talk and socialize, and I often get my emotional

Embracing Support

bank account filled socializing with her. She's very funny and a great person to talk to. However, if I let it, this socializing can interfere with my work, so I take control of the situation and consciously choose when to socialize. For example, she knows that when I'm on my way to class, I don't have the time to talk. So, if I rush by and simply wave at her, she doesn't take it personally. Having boundaries in the social area can be just as important as socializing when it comes to internal support.

Here are a few questions you can ask yourself to discover whether or not you are supporting your social well-being:

- ∞ What do you believe is the purpose of social interaction?
- ∞ Do you feel like you're a part of your neighbourhood/community?
- ∞ Are you tolerant and accepting of others?
- ∞ How do you feel about meeting new people? Are you open to talking to strangers?
- ∞ What role do you play when socializing? (E.g. primarily listen, primarily speak, both equally, etc.). Do you ever challenge yourself to take on a different role than what you usually take?
- ∞ How do you feel after socializing as part of a group?
- ∞ How do you feel just before you go to meet a group of people?
- ∞ Is it challenging for you to meet new people?
- ∞ What is your motivation when socializing?
- ∞ What feels like the safest form of socializing? The riskiest?
- ∞ What is the scariest part about social

interactions?
∞ What did you learn about socializing while growing up? Who did you learn this from?
∞ Do you limit who you're willing to socialize with?
∞ When you socialize, do you feel like you are able to contribute to the welfare of others?
∞ How big is your social network?
∞ How many close friends do you have that you can confide in?
∞ When you need to talk to someone about a problem, how many people could you call on?
∞ If you needed someone to help you move your home, how many people could you call on?

Now return to the Seven Domains of Internal Support Diagram and take a few minutes to write down the types of social internal support you currently participate in and, if applicable, how often.

"Be who you are and say what you feel because those who mind don't matter and those who matter don't mind."
∞ ***Dr. Seuss*** ∞

Activity: Pulling it all Together

I hope you now have a clear picture of the internal support you currently create for yourself—and an idea of which domains of internal support you would benefit from expanding on. The following activity encourages you to build on the notes you made on the Seven Domains of Internal Support Diagram.

Embracing Support

1. Review the diagram and reflect on or summarize what you currently do to support yourself. What steps do you take to make yourself feel more empowered and purposeful? What makes you feel like you love and respect yourself? Do you notice any patterns?

   _____
   _____
   _____
   _____
   _____
   _____
   _____

2. Would you like to create more internal support in any of the seven domains (physical, intellectual/mental, emotional, spiritual, financial/occupational, environmental, or social)? What specifically will you do to feel more balance in the domains that are lacking?

   _____
   _____
   _____
   _____
   _____
   _____
   _____

3. For each of the Seven Domains of Internal Support, list five more ways you could create

more love, support, and respect for yourself, which you are not currently doing.

∞ Physical

_____
_____
_____

∞ Intellectual/Mental

_____
_____
_____

∞ Emotional

_____
_____
_____

∞ Spiritual

_____
_____
_____

∞ Financial/Occupational

_____
_____
_____

Embracing Support

∞ Environmental

_____
_____
_____
_____

∞ Social

_____
_____
_____
_____

4. Read through your responses to Question 3 and highlight or circle at least one of the new choices you can commit to right now, every day for the next four weeks. Commit to making the time and setting boundaries to ensure it happens, even if it's just for a little while. Don't get caught up on, "I don't have an hour to exercise right now." Even five minutes of singing or dancing will make a huge difference in your energy level and set you on the path to a longer time commitment. What are you willing to commit to? Make a plan.

_____
_____
_____
_____
_____
_____
_____

5. Ask for support! Remember that every little thing brings you a step closer to having greater internal support. If you need help, now is a great time to ask for external support so you can create internal support for yourself. Who will you ask for external support? What will you ask them for? Use the "act as if" approach if it helps you get focused.

_____
_____
_____
_____
_____
_____

6. Be accountable for your choices. If you decide not to follow through, what will the consequences be for your lack of accountability? Also think about the beliefs you will be reinforcing by not following through.

_____
_____
_____
_____
_____
_____

7. What support will you access to help you stay accountable to yourself and continue to follow through?

Embracing Support

_____
_____
_____
_____
_____
_____
_____

Celebrate Success

Let's celebrate your commitment to internal support. One of the most important things you can do is celebrate your success, especially after completing self-reflection such as this. Many of us don't commemorate our achievements enough or don't know how to, for countless reasons and underlying beliefs. If giving yourself credit for your achievements is a challenge for you, I encourage you to revisit and work through some of the previous activities to discover the beliefs that may be limiting you from celebrating. If you've never learned how to celebrate, now is a great time to practice, and by watching how others do it, you can choose how you would like to celebrate your own successes.

Think about all the ways in which you could celebrate the learning, new insights, and the changes you have decided to make by committing to internal support. Sing, dance, make music, call a friend, go for coffee, make time to socialize, buy yourself something, give this book as a gift to a friend, allow quiet time for yourself, go out to a club or out for a meal, or whatever you prefer to do. Take a few minutes and write down as many of your own ideas as you can think of. Do any of them create more internal support?

_____
_____
_____
_____
_____

Now make a point of actually following through on one of your celebration ideas. Do it with the clear intent of celebrating your success at completing this book and at the new insights you have gained. Celebrate your abundance and the fact that you can think and read. Celebrate your friends, your family, your new support system. Celebrate change and celebrate life. Whatever you choose, celebrate each day. **The more you celebrate the abundance you see in your life, the more abundance you'll have**. You deserve it.

So, What Have We Learned?

Congratulations! You have reached the end of the Internal Support Strategy.

In this chapter:
- ✓ We've defined internal support.
- ✓ We've looked at how our beliefs may cause us to sacrifice internal support to support others.
- ✓ We've discussed "sharpening the saw" to impact internal support and self-care.
- ✓ We've reflected on how much internal

Embracing Support

support you currently create.
- ✓ We've looked at some examples of how we can increase internal support through our actions and attitudes, and by setting priorities.
- ✓ We've discussed the Seven Domains of Internal Support and how to create more balance in self-care and internal support.
- ✓ We've addressed the importance of celebrating success and abundance.

By exploring what you already do to support yourself in each of these areas, you are better able to increase the amount of internal support you have, and to understand how to access the right kind of external support to get you to where you want to be. Now is a great time to commit to more internal support for yourself, as you journey to having the external support you need to live a happy, empowered, amazing life.

"You yourself, as much as anybody in the entire universe, deserve your love and affection."

∞ **Buddha** ∞

Every End Is a New Beginning

When one door closes, another opens; but we often look so long and so regretfully upon the closed door that we do not see the one which has opened for us.
∞ **Alexander Graham Bell** ∞

I want to thank you, dear reader. I hope that reading this book and playing along through the exercises has been as helpful to you as the writing of it has been to me. It took a long time before this book finally came to fruition, primarily because I let my own beliefs get in my way. When I started to write it, I was very excited about the process and about starting my own coaching and seminar venture. I was so excited that I wrote about half of the contents in a matter of weeks. Then my beliefs kicked in and began to stall the process. I thought, "I can't do this. I'm not good enough. I have nothing of value to offer."

Those beliefs were so loud and interfered so much that they led to seven years of excuses, explanations, and justifications for not finishing: "I'm too busy at work. I don't have time to write with everything going on with work and my kids." "My mom is ill, and I have to take care of her." "My mom passed away, I'm grieving, and I can't be a support to myself, never mind anyone else." "I don't think I want to be a business owner anymore." "I'm too depressed to write." "I don't care anymore and who do I think I am to do something of this magnitude?" But this all changed when I finally reached out and asked for, accepted, and

Embracing Support

allowed external support to keep me moving.

Every time I'd get stuck, I started using all of the tools, activities, and examples that I have included in these pages, and I'd reach out to my coaches, peers, and editors to help keep me moving forward. When I'd get stuck and decide I couldn't do it, or that there was no value in this information, I'd get a sign from my students, my patients, or my peers that, "Yes! I'm not the only one struggling." So I kept moving forward, and I learned more about support, and the importance of acting as if.

As I wrote each section, I had tremendous new insights into various areas of my life, and I hope you have had similar deep and meaningful experiences. Some of them may have been a bit scary (or downright terrifying—as they were for me), and that's okay. That's what happens when we challenge our beliefs. Remember to be gentle with yourself as you learn new ways of being and learn how to apply these new strategies in your life. Completing the activities will impact your life, and the depth of your commitment to creating empowerment will affect the extent of the results. You have gained some amazing new insights through self-reflection in this book to help you become more loved, empowered, and purposeful. Celebrate your successes.

As you've learned, the amazing thing about asking for support is that once you get clear on what you want, finding the right person to provide that support gets really easy. If you're clear on what you want and then ask for support, you'll know right away if this is the right person to give you that support. If they're not, keep looking and over time and with practice you'll start seeking support in people you wouldn't ever have thought to ask. By being open to the experience of asking for and receiving (accepting and allowing) support, amazing things can happen.

On a short side note, finding professional support isn't always as difficult or as expensive as it might seem. Many professions require students to do a practicum with real people, and sometimes the general public is asked to participate. For example, massage therapy students at one of our local universities partake in supervised practice on real people, and this is a wonderful opportunity for someone to receive a massage and possibly some health advice at a much reduced cost. To access resources such as these, all you need to do is pick up the phone or search online.

Remember that you have an abundance of resources available to you as you continue to live your new choices. You have external support available when you choose to look for and access it, and you have new tools to help you create more internal support. Be sure to check out my website www.healwithsupport.com for additional support resources in the form of books, online tools, and activities to help you keep practicing to change unsupportive thoughts and beliefs and create new, more supportive thought patterns.

Writing this book has had an incredible impact on my perspective of support, and in turn, my life. I hope that by reading it you have also seen this value. Having support is a powerful tool for living better, loving more, and making dreams happen. Thank you for allowing my dream to happen. I wish you much love and support on your journey to a happy, empowered, amazing life. Remember, you're never without support. You just have to embrace it. You have the resources now, you have an abundance of support available to you, and you have the power within you. Make it happen for yourself. Take charge, and create your Happy, Empowered, Amazing Life with support. Now is the time to HEAL.

"You see things; and you say, 'Why?'
But I dream things that never were; and I say,
'Why not?'"
∞ ***George Bernard Shaw*** ∞

In Honor of My Mom

Throughout this book I have told many stories of my life and growing up in a single parent household as an immigrant family. My mom had some tremendous challenges to overcome to care for the three of us, and I know her beliefs about what life should have been like weighed heavily on her. I also know she always did the best that she could with the tools and information she had. I tell these stories, not as a strike against my mom's parenting skills, but rather from a place of growth and realization as to why I am the person I am today. There were many times we argued, hurt each other's feelings, were angry with each other, or didn't speak for weeks on end. Then there were other times when we were incredibly close, and my mom was my best friend and biggest supporter.

I unconsciously took on the responsibility to care for her, as far back as I can remember. Probably back to the time when my sister was born. In 1993, when I graduated from nursing school and there were no nursing jobs in Alberta because of government cutbacks, rather than look abroad for work, I decided to stay in Canada and take on a non-nursing job so I could stay close to her and take care of her (even though she did not need me to on any level). I remember telling a friend I would rather miss out on opportunities elsewhere so I could be close by in case something happened to my mom, than to have the best job in the world and not be there for her if she needed me. Over time though, as you might guess, this was not the best decision for a 21-year-old with the world at her fingertips. Even though it was my choice to do so,

Embracing Support

I resented the unconscious responsibility right from the start.

In 2007, when my mom was initially diagnosed with colon cancer and was afflicted by her stroke, I was a new mom with a three-year-old and a three-week-old baby. Because I was the oldest, because I was a nurse, and because I had always done so, the responsibility of Mom's care naturally gravitated to me, and because I didn't know how to ask for and accept support, the resentment grew, and I started down the path to burnout. You've heard this story before.

Over time we managed, and Mom was successfully back on her feet, even though she was no longer able to drive. She had an amazing support network to help her get around, and she was able to stay on the farm (an hour and a half away from where I live) independently. And she travelled. She went to Switzerland several times, on two or three cruises, as well as to South America, to Mexico, and twice to the Dominican Republic to spend her winters. She really was an amazing lady.

On her return from her last trip to the Dominican, we knew something was wrong, and because I'm a palliative care nurse, I knew exactly what. My instincts told me this was the beginning of the end. She was able to make one final trip to Switzerland to see her family before she was hospitalized and underwent radiation treatments for a recurrent tumor in her groin area which was cutting off the lymph circulation to her leg and causing her a tremendous amount of pain and swelling.

For my part, I was working, I was busy with my family, and now I had all of these additional hospital visits and doctors' appointments to add to my schedule. For a time I was my mom's primary caregiver in my own home. My sister came and helped out with what she could, but eventually my mom's care became more than either of us were willing or capable of handling. I still have tremendous guilt over not taking the time off work or making different arrangements so I could have spent this time with my mom. For not taking the time or making a bigger effort, I am eternally sorry.

However, I also recognize that keeping my distance was a way to protect myself from the pain of losing her, which I knew full well was coming closer each day. Instinctively I knew we would lose Mom before the end of the summer. Unfortunately, I was right. At the beginning of August 2011, Mom was admitted to the Palliative Hospice at the Edmonton General Hospital and received incredible care there. We will forever be grateful for the amazing team of nurses, caregivers and physicians on the unit.

On the night before Mom left us, I was debating if I should go to the hospital. Instincts again told me that I should go, but I decided to go in the morning instead. I got a phone call about half an hour after I made that decision letting me know that Mom's breathing had changed and that perhaps I'd like to come in and be with her. I went and sat with her and told her everything would be okay. I told her I'd look after things and take care of what needed to be done, just as I always had. When she was fighting for breath, I told her it was okay to stop fighting and to let go. And I was there and held her hand when she took her last breath.

True to my word, I took the reins and ruled the

Embracing Support

Kingdom of I Can Do it All by Myself, and did what needed to be done. We settled an extremely challenging estate, planned and prepared the funeral in Canada as well as back in Switzerland, and I was the rock I always had been to make sure every last detail had been taken care of. I refused help. I just wanted to get it over and done with. At every turn something came up to make the process even more challenging. Still, I didn't ask for or accept support.

About six months after Mom passed, I went into a depression that immobilized me for several weeks. I went to work, did what I had to do, and nothing more. At home, I barely made it through my day, and I am so thankful for my husband for stepping up and looking after things with the kids and around the house. My time at home consisted of me sitting on the couch, staring at the TV, or sleeping. It was almost two months before I started doing things for myself again, before I felt like living again. During this time, my support system really came through for me.

Even with all of this emotional turmoil, I was able to function normally on an intellectual level, somewhat in complete denial about the whole thing; until the anger surfaced. Then I was angry all the time and life was so frustrating, because nothing worked the way it was supposed to. January to April of 2013 were some of the most frustrating months I've experienced, because every little thing would just set off my anger. Again, intellectually, I knew this was part of grieving, but I just couldn't find my way through it. Until I went back to Switzerland in April of 2013.

One day on that trip, I took my kids for a walk around my Swiss home town. I showed them the hospital where I was born and later worked for two months the summer before I started nursing school. I showed them where I went to school and where we used to live. I took them out to the old ruin from Roman times, and we walked past my grandma's old house and the little church where I used to go as a small child. I shared my memories about the town and I taught my kids the meaning of the chimes of the church bells. Finally, we went to the cemetery to meet up with my sister, and to bring flowers for my grandparents, and of course for Mom. I could feel my anger was still there, but this trip around town with all the memories had softened it, as had bringing the flowers.

The most amazing thing, however, happened on the flight back to Canada. As exhausted as I was, sitting on an airplane from Toronto to Edmonton, my mind created a powerful image for me and as I dozed off, gave me the most remarkable dream. I saw myself back in my home town on a beautiful, warm summer day. I met many people I knew, and although I couldn't see their faces, I knew who they were just by their light and their energy. My aunt, who is still alive, was there, but so were my grandparents, both of whom have passed on, along with several other people I haven't seen in a very long time. We exchanged a few words and hugs, and one-by-one they disappeared, until only one person remained. Slowly, she came into view in my dream. The light was bright and warm and I could finally make out my mom, young and healthy, wearing a white summer shirt and bright yellow shorts. She came closer and became clearer and when she spoke I also heard my own voice say, "thank you." We both said: "Thank you for looking after me, for taking me to appointments, for sacrificing time away from the kids." We thanked each other for all the things I had been so angry and resentful about. And just as she thanked me, I also thanked her for all her time and sacrifice in raising us by herself. One-by-one they all got listed and spoken, and with each "thank you" the energy became brighter and I felt lighter and more forgiving. I came back to a wakeful consciousness and realized I was speaking out loud and tears were streaming down my face. I felt like it was finally over, and I could now focus on living my life with love and forgiveness.

    This story comes full circle about three weeks after this dream, as I went to a writers' conference and learned about how to write query letters and approach publishers with manuscripts. I had a break between sessions and decided to nurture my soul with a swim. As usual, I cleared my head while swimming and came up with several solutions to problems that had been weighing on me the previous day. As I was sitting in the hot tub afterwards, I realized just why everything was coming together so nicely and why I now had this amazing life where I am able to write and create and live exactly the way I want to. It all came back to 25 years earlier when my mom said to me, "Get an education so you can get a good job and have enough money to make your dreams come true." Well, I did, and I am. So, thank you, Mom, for having that incredible insight then and for pushing me into a career I now love, even though I didn't want to be a nurse at the time. I am now exactly where I need to be—to be, do, and have everything that I ever dreamed about. It's finally all coming together, and it's because of all of

the lessons, beliefs, and values I learned from my mom, and because she taught me to keep striving for better until it's right. I love you Mom. And I will forever be grateful.
 —me

"Death isn't sad. The sad thing is: most people don't live at all."

∞ ***Socrates*** ∞
The Peaceful Warrior (Film)

References and Resources

Arntz, W., Chasse, B., Hoffman, M., & Vicente, M. (Writers). (2004). *What tнē #$*! D̄ө ωΣ (k)πow!?* Captured Light/Lord of the Wind Production.

Canfield, J. (2005/2007). *How to get from where you are to where you want to be: The 25 principles of success.* Hammersmith, London: Harper Element of HarperCollins Publishers Ltd.

Covey, S.R. (1989). *The 7 habits of highly effective people: Restoring the character ethic.* New York: Simon & Schuster.

Casey, S. (2012). *Belief Re-patterning: The amazing technique for "flipping the switch" to positive thoughts.* Carlsbad, CA: Hay House, Inc.

Deutschman, A. (2007). *Change or die: The three keys to change at work and in life.* New York: HarperCollins Publishers Ltd.

Emery, S. (1977). *Actualizations: You don't have to rehearse to be yourself.* Garden City, NY: Doubleday & Company, Inc.

Fiset, J. (2007). *Reframe your blame: How to be personally accountable.* Calgary, AB: Personal Best Publications.

Hay, L.L. (1999). *You can heal your life.* Carlsbad, CA: Hay House Inc.

Jampolsky, G.G. (1979). *Love is letting go of fear.* Berkley, CA: Celestial Arts.

Losier, M.J. (2003). *Law of attraction: The science of attracting more of what you want and less of what you don't.* Victoria, BC: Michael J. Losier.

Millman, D. (2006). *Way of the peaceful warrior: A*

book that changes lives. Tiburon, CA: H J Kramer/New World Library.

Potter, P. A., Perry, A. G., Stockert, A. P., & Hall, A. M. (2019). *Canadian fundamentals of nursing.* (B. J. Astle & W. Duggleby, Eds.) (6th ed.). Toronto: Elsevier Canada, a division of Reed Elsevier Canada, Ltd.

Robbins, A. (1992). *Awaken the giant within: How to take immediate control of your mental, emotional, physical and financial destiny!* New York: Free Press.

Thompson, V.D. (2019). *Health and health care delivery in* Canada (3rd ed.). Toronto: Elsevier Canada.

Training Fleas. (2006, November 7). Retrieved 2019, from https://www.youtube.com/watch?v=GlpjA-QgmQM.

About the Author

Claudia is a Registered Nurse with over 25 years of experience, both as a university nursing instructor and as an acute palliative care nurse. She started working on her master's in adult education while on maternity leave with her first baby and after completion went on to coach, counsel, and support countless students, peers, patients, and families. As a result, she has learned to embrace support in her own life. Through her unique perspective on the importance of asking for, accepting, and allowing support, she is able to empower and inspire those who work with her. Claudia is a happily married working mom of two teenage girls who spends her leisure time reading, writing, and creating. With the support of her amazing friends and family, she gets to live her passions every day.

"Do not go where the path may lead,
go instead where there is no path
and leave a trail."
∞ *Ralph Waldo Emerson* ∞

www.ingramcontent.com/pod-product-compliance
Lightning Source LLC
Chambersburg PA
CBHW071954070526
44583CB00015B/1187